D0382101

# Lessons from
# Private Equity
# Any Company
# Can Use

# Publisher's Note: Memo to the CEO

Authored by leading experts and examining issues of special urgency, the books in the Memo to the CEO series are tailored for today's time-starved executives. Concise, focused, and solutions-oriented, each book explores a critical management challenge and offers authoritative counsel, provocative points of view, and practical insight.

Also available:

# Lessons from Private Equity Any Company Can Use

## Orit Gadiesh
## Hugh MacArthur

Bain & Company, Inc.

Harvard Business Press
Boston, Massachusetts

No part of this publication may be reproduced, stored in or introduced into
a retrieval system, or transmitted, in any form, or by any means (electronic,
mechanical, photocopying, recording, or otherwise), without the prior
permission of the publisher. Requests for permission should be directed to
permissions@hbsp.harvard.edu, or mailed to Permissions, Harvard Business
School Publishing, 60 Harvard Way, Boston, Massachusetts 02163.

Gadiesh, Orit.

    Lessons from private equity any company can use / Orit Gadiesh, Hugh
MacArthur.

      p.   cm.

    ISBN 978-1-4221-2495-6

    1. Private equity. 2. Venture capital. 3. Investments. I. MacArthur, Hugh.
II. Title.

HG4751.G33   2008

658.15'224—dc22

                                                               2007036567

The paper used in this publication meets the requirements of the American
National Standard for Permanence of Paper for Publications and Documents in
Libraries and Archives Z39.48-1992

# Contents

# Introducing the
# Private Equity Advantage

Private equity (PE) has dominated the business headlines in recent years. Once a relatively low-profile, even exotic industry, it has moved into a significant position in the U.S. economy, is playing a prominent role in the rest of the developed economies around the world, and is quickly assuming more importance in some of the largest and fastest-growing developing markets.

As the first management consulting firm to develop a global PE practice, Bain & Company has quite literally grown up with the industry. Today, our practice is the largest of its kind. We conduct detailed strategic due diligence on hundreds of targets annually and work in depth with portfolio companies and their management teams to boost performance. We are not simply on the outside looking in, either. Bain & Company partners have invested over $500 million of their own capital in private equity funds and deals over the last few years, with top-quartile results.

From a very granular and unique perspective, we have come to understand what PE leaders are particularly good at, and also what they are not so good at, as it pertains to creating more valuable companies.

So what is this memo about? It's about how to make businesses more valuable, regardless of who owns them. While much has been written on this topic, and no memo, however well intentioned, will provide a panacea for value creation to all executives across all industries, we feel strongly from our many years of working with the best PE executives and the most capable chief executive officers that the PE industry can offer some general lessons that any business leader should consider to get the most out of his or her business.

Having worked with thousands of CEOs of public and private companies, we fully realize that some CEOs have used the same approach to the topic we will be discussing without ever having looked at PE firms, and that others have taken PE lessons to heart some time ago. This memo may serve mainly as a tool for propagating them. Some leaders may be aware of PE lessons but face challenges in employing them. We hope to offer clear, practical suggestions for implementation. Some may not yet have faced the issues raised here, and we hope we articulate both the lessons and their application in ways that are helpful.

In short, some of these lessons will sound familiar. Some may even appear obvious. However, in our view they are not being consistently and rigorously applied by businesses around the world. We see two main reasons for this: first, the application of these lessons drives real change in many businesses, and, for better or worse, change brings risks, both real and imagined. There is validity to the old truism about people disliking change. Second, many leaders apply the lessons that we will discuss, but incompletely. It is easier to do "fine" than to do the "best" a company can do. We call this *satisfactory underperformance*—a pervasive disease in business that is the direct target of this memo.

Your most important task as a leader is to *make your company more valuable*. Most studies confirm that the *best* PE investors do exactly that: they generate excellent returns on their investments, usually after a period of ownership of three to five years. In this memo, we not only will further explain these results, but also will describe *how* these PE investors achieve them, and why their approach is relevant to all companies, regardless of ownership structure.

At the same time, a leader is committed to creating opportunities and rewards for the people who help make the company successful. Several studies have concluded that in the markets most thoroughly penetrated by PE players, job creation by PE-controlled firms significantly outpaces job creation in the rest of the economy.[1]

These are two of the most compelling reasons for you to take note of the success of the best PE firms and to figure out which of their tools and techniques you might adopt for yourself. How can you create more value for your shareholders, and more opportunities (in the form of jobs, financial rewards, and promotions) for your star performers? How can you combine these outcomes to form a results-oriented culture for all of your productive employees?

Take, for example, the story of Crown Castle, an owner-operator of shared wireless infrastructure that PE firm Berkshire Partners invested in and expanded by acquiring transmission towers from wireless carriers. In 1998, Crown Castle went public, garnering Berkshire a tenfold return on its initial investment. As a public company, Crown Castle maintained many of the lessons we will discuss, such as regularly reevaluating the full potential of its business and focusing the organization on pursuing a crucial handful of initiatives to achieve its full potential. Revenues increased sevenfold, and the workforce grew 40 percent—under the continuous leadership of CEO John Kelly and CFO Ben Moreland. Wall Street applauded, and the company's stock price outperformed the S&P 500 by a factor of more than two, from its IPO in 1998 through the end of October 2007. Crown Castle's story should give all senior managers comfort: the lessons in this memo can work inside or outside the PE portfolio.

So, what are these lessons? We characterize them as follows:

- Define the full potential.

- Develop the blueprint.

- Accelerate performance.

- Harness the talent.

- Make equity sweat.

- Foster a results-oriented mind-set.

No single private equity firm that we know consistently applies all of these disciplines to every single investment. There are some real examples, too, of PE firms ignoring long-term operating value to turn a quick profit. However, despite the press's trumpeting about asset stripping and debt overload, these instances are far fewer than the noise would suggest. Rather, there is an intense focus by the best PE investors, on whose practices this memo is based, to develop repeatable, sustainable processes that make their companies more valuable over time.

Market forces, competition, debt conditions, currency values, and regulation will all cycle up and down during the course of investments. The smartest PE investors have realized that the only way to reliably increase the value of their portfolios is to maximize the operating value of the underlying businesses in them. For this reason, the best PE firms have shifted many of the resources that they once poured into financial engineering toward creating operating value—and they are doing it in a way that is more systematic, focused, and aggressive than the practices found in most companies. The need to provide strong returns to demanding limited partners (LPs) in a defined time frame creates a single-mindedness that fuels the rigor with which these lessons are applied.

If you are not the clear-cut market leader in your industry, you can't afford to ignore how the best PE firms are transforming the business landscape. Even if you are the clear-cut leader, our research has shown that such companies oftentimes perform below their true, full potential, and examining the full measure of these lessons can benefit them greatly.

# What Is Going On in Private Equity?

Active investing has set a new standard—one that senior corporate leaders should evaluate and aspire to. Private equity, in particular, is changing the rules of the game. Why does PE matter to the broader corporate world? There are several answers.

There is a veritable flood of money out there, looking to be invested profitably. Part of the flood is owing to the fact that global pensions, institutional endowments, insurance company assets, and other sources of limited partner capital have been growing at record rates and are at all-time highs. In just the past three years, new fund-raising rounds by PE firms have brought in more than \$1 trillion of capital globally—more than was raised cumulatively in the industry's history. Add the leverage provided by lenders, and that adds up to several trillions of dollars of buying power.

Why have so many PE firms been successful at raising capital? The short answer is that the *best* PE firms offer investors the opportunity to earn superior returns, in good times and in bad. And we are careful to use the phrase *the best*. Although the research is still somewhat murky, it appears that over the long term, *average* PE returns (net of fees) may only equal those of public markets. (Some academics have made the case that the S&P 500 consistently outperforms the average PE fund. Others have recently suggested that the average PE fund earns more from management fees than from increasing the value of their companies.) So this distinction between the *average* and the *best* is critical, and it's definitely worth digging down into the details.

Looking at American buyout funds raised between 1969 and 2006, you will find that the returns for the bottom-quartile funds were all negative. If we're looking for a yellow "caution" flag, there it is. But what about the top performers? The top-quartile funds enjoyed internal rates of return (IRRs) of 36 percent on average, with some earning triple-digit rates of returns. That's year in and year out. By comparison, the top-quartile companies that were part of the S&P 500 as of year-end 2006 have generated annual shareholder returns of 28 percent on average, from the time they went public. And unlike mutual fund com-

panies—whose performances vary widely over time—
the best PE firms achieve superior returns consistently across all their funds over time. Phrased slightly
differently, PE firms managing a top-performing fund
have a significantly above-average chance of having
their next fund also feature in the top performers.

As a result—not surprisingly—the best PE firms
are getting bigger. Today, most of the new money goes
not to the mediocre players, but to the multibillion-
dollar megafunds that have delivered consistently
strong returns for their investors. However, it is important to note that these huge new pools of money
will provide megafunds with challenges in creating
comparable future performance. More and larger
funds mean larger transaction sizes and higher prices
as the market becomes increasingly competitive.

While increasing global liquidity and attractive returns explain the *supply* side of the PE equation, there
are also drivers on the *demand* side that make PE
ownership attractive for those that manage companies. One such issue may surprise: increased control
over one's fate. PE ownership can give companies
the freedom to strike a balance between entrepre-
neurship on the one hand and financial discipline on
the other. The right balance can vary widely by
industry and country, but most observers would
agree that many public companies tend to err on the

side of shortsightedness. They also tend to favor the short term over the long term and the conservative strategy over the bold departure.

PE also offers companies a different and attractive approach to governance at a time when remaining a publicly held company entails a whole spectrum of new hard and soft costs, and also imposes structural constraints. Senior executives of public companies are only too familiar with the costly strictures of Sarbanes-Oxley in the United States, Higgs in the United Kingdom, and their equivalents in many other Western economies. They are also aware of their increased personal liability in today's regulatory environment. But less has been written on those pay-for-performance plans that really do drive value in the PE context, or the more efficient board structure that helps a company take action swiftly and adds real value to a management team. In many cases, these same tools and structures can be carried into traditional corporate settings, giving CEOs at those companies substantially more running room.

Next, PE is being used by developed markets to help reform uncompetitive industries and social structures—as, for example, in Blackstone's 2006 investment in Deutsche Telekom (DT), whereby the German government is tacitly allowing Blackstone to push through restructuring and cost reduction to make DT more viable and efficient.

Lastly, PE is also being used by developing countries to accelerate economic growth. PE has played a critical role in developing the Indian mobile telecom market, which is now the fastest growing in the world; China's 2004 sale of 18 percent of the Shenzen Development Bank to Newbridge Capital was conceived in exactly the same spirit.[2] In the developing world, PE is a tool not only for private business, but also for governments seeking to learn useful lessons and apply them to current economic problems.

Thanks to these trends, the PE approach will continue to be relevant for the foreseeable future. The industry will no doubt continue to go through its cycles of ups and downs. As anyone who reads the financial press is well aware, there have been challenges to specific deals, as well as challenges within specific markets. These kinds of episodes and the controversy they can provoke will recur.

But three central facts remain: first, PE has become a major force in global financial markets. With trillions of dollars of PE capital afloat, neither tax legislation nor public criticism is likely to reverse the long-term trend toward PE ownership of more assets on a global basis.

Second, the best PE firms have set a concrete and inescapable benchmark for global business performance. There is clearly something in the PE formula that is working. By following a half-dozen deceptively simple rules, the leading players in the PE community create value to a degree that many traditional companies do not—or at least have not, to date.

Third, short-term fluctuations in credit markets and economic cycles aside (such as the subprime credit panic of the summer of 2007), hardly any company escapes consideration as a PE takeover target. Consider, for example, Canadian telecommunications operator BCE, which was taken over by an Ontario pension fund and two American PE firms for $48.5 billion. No brand, no matter how iconic, is out of reach: Chrysler (bought by Cerberus Capital), Ducati motorcycles (TPG), Tiffany (Investcorp), Gucci (Investcorp), and Neiman Marcus (TPG and Warburg Pincus). The list goes on and on: Hertz, Hilton Hotels, Metro-Goldwyn-Mayer, and EMI Group. With increasing scale, scope, and speed, PE firms are assembling portfolios that have turned them into some of the world's biggest conglomerates.

Meanwhile, the kinds of red flags that in the past might have scared off potential PE suitors are losing their power to intimidate. PE firms used to steer clear of stranded assets and labor entanglements, for example, but these issues no longer seem to be the powerful disincentives that they once were. Chrysler's sale even had the initial support of the autoworkers' union. "The transaction with Cerberus," the president of the United Auto Workers (UAW) told the *Detroit Free Press*, "is in the best interests of our UAW members, the Chrysler Group, and Daimler."[3] The UAW settled a fall 2007 wage dispute with Chrysler within one day.

Of course, you have not only PE firms, but also hedge funds in the game—buying effective control of companies, if not buying them entirely, sometimes even on a hostile basis. It's a new world out there.

# How Can PE Lessons
# Apply to You?

Many smart companies—their top executives and their boards—are reviewing the PE case and asking a key question: what would we do differently if we had a PE mind-set?

Peter Brabeck-Letmathe, CEO of Nestlé, asked this question when he took the company's helm in 1997. While he saw stark differences between his company's aim to nurture, grow, and renew products over decades versus a PE firm's aim to buy a mature business, boost operational value, and sell, he nonetheless found many applications of PE disciplines and has ridden them to one of the most consistent, long-term track records in his sector. Compared to other large, diversified food companies—the pool in which Nestlé competes—the Swiss food and beverage maker has outstroked its rivals; during Brabeck's tenure over the past ten years Nestlé has grown market capitalization 3.5 times, to more than SF 200 billion, and delivered total shareholder returns in excess of 15 percent annually.

In the following pages, we will return frequently to Nestlé as an exemplar of a public company that has and is applying PE's six key lessons. We'll also cite examples of a number of firms transformed by private equity ownership. We will make the case that any company can accelerate its value in much the same way, without a PE buyer. The private equity lens and its defined investment horizon merely provide the clearest view of how these lessons work. But to effect any transformation in your business, you have to be willing to challenge people in your organization and probably your board, and let them challenge you—all with the imperative of focusing your organization maniacally, relentlessly, and zealously on results. This is accomplished through a rigorous application of six main lessons:

- **Define the full potential:** To improve profits and stock price, you need to make strategic choices with a clear picture of the *full potential* of your company in mind. Full potential is not about next year's budget, and it is certainly not a strategic plan that takes current trends, overlays them with "aspirations," and melds them into what often amounts to a picture that distorts a company's true potential. Instead, defining the full potential of your business is rigorously asking and factually answering the question "How high is up?" The target is increased equity value—how do you turn $1 of equity value today into $3, $4, or $5 tomorrow? "Strategic due diligence" is the way to set the number, and growing your cash flow by pursuing a few core initiatives derived from this due diligence is the way to get there. Here is the key concept: *no company can be successful when it divides its resources among too many initiatives*. Focusing on the right critical issues—no more than three to five, in most cases—is crucial to achieving success.[4]

In Nestlé's case, Brabeck had a target of substantially improving the value of the company by increasing organic growth to 5 to 6 percent together with continuously improving margins and targeting an industry-outperforming total shareholder return of 300 percent. He then mapped out four "pillars" of value creation to transform his company from one focused on agro-business into one vested in research and development–led nutrition. These pillars—operational performance improvement; innovating and renovating the product portfolio; broadening distribution to reach customers "whenever, wherever, however"; and strengthening consumer communications—laid the foundation for change.

Adopting such a focus necessarily will encourage a more medium-term outlook. Wittingly or unwittingly, every company locates itself somewhere on the spectrum of performance improvement: from the short-term focus (i.e., quarterly) to the indefinite term (i.e., infinity). In most cases, as it turns out, the practical, actionable time frame for getting to full potential is three to five years: in other words, a private equity investor's typical time frame.

• **Develop the blueprint:** The blueprint is the road map for getting to that full-potential destination—the *who, what, when, where,* and *how.* In most cases, the blueprint zeroes in on the few initiatives you identified in the full-potential thesis: the ones that will create the most value for the company in the medium term. What is a blueprint? Nothing more and nothing less than a strategic operating plan that takes those key initiatives and turns them into results. The emphasis is on measurable actions. It starts with high-level moves and works its way down to things you can actually do differently on "Monday morning, at 8 a.m." —in other words, to the detailed operational level—choreographing the moves from standing start to the finish line. Along the way, it helps create excitement and build alignment.

Taking just one of Nestlé's critical initiatives—operational performance improvement—the blueprint called first for taking fat out of current operations, which netted $3 billion of savings in three years. It then involved retooling the business platform by collapsing dozens of enterprise resource planning (ERP) systems across multiple business units into one and establishing a common system design and template for the company's global operations while still allowing differences for local markets. The effort, called Global Business Excellence, or GLOBE, has transformed Nestlé, in Brabeck's own words, from being run "like a supertanker" into an "agile fleet" that calls different business units into action to penetrate different product, customer, or geographic segments, and shares best practices across campaigns.[5] In the process, Nestlé has enabled growth and further improvements in operational productivity.

- **Accelerate performance:** Once your priorities
  are identified and blocked out through the blueprint, the overriding goal becomes to *accelerate
  the performance* of your company. True, most
  companies embrace what they perceive to be
  far-reaching targets and lay out big initiatives.
  But without driving organizational change
  around the key initiatives that will define success, many of these firms fall short of their
  goals. In part, this means molding the organization to the blueprint and matching talent to
  key initiatives. It also means getting people to
  own the key initiatives, and setting up appropriate program management tools to support
  the initiatives and their "owners." Importantly,
  Nestlé's Brabeck gave Chris Johnson, a fast-
  rising *business unit* executive—not an IT
  executive—accountability for GLOBE's results.

  Finally, accelerating performance means
  monitoring a few key metrics. These metrics
  go well beyond the deep pools of standard
  management accounting data—for the most
  part, backward looking and nonactionable. To
  look into the future, other kinds of information
  are required, especially certain kinds of market
  and operational data. When you track the most
  critical data, you are in a position to determine

whether the business is moving in the right direction or not. Your blueprint determines the key measures that are required to track the success of the chosen initiatives; the company then drives the entire corporate language and rewards system around those metrics.

- **Harness the talent:** The best-laid plans go nowhere without the right people to implement them. All companies need great people throughout the management structure, and need them to think like owners. This means that you have to use the right incentives to recruit, retain, and motivate these talented folks. (Every type of corporate owner is competing for exactly the same kind of talent. Money alone won't cut it—culture, too, is key—but in many cases, money is the first hurdle that you have to get over.) Why have corporate stars like IBM's Lou Gerstner and GE's Jack Welch wound up with second careers in private equity? Why did GE superstar David Calhoun jump ship in the summer of 2006 to become CEO of the VNU Group (now The Nielsen Company), a Dutch company that was acquired by a PE consortium in 2006? Why are so many senior corporate managers today tapping into their networks of contacts to get introductions to deal makers? Because in the typical PE environment, the rewards are higher and the bureaucracy is less onerous. Many talented managers want both to do the right thing by shareholders *and* to reap their just rewards.

But public companies can also compete for top talent. Nestlé, for example, introduced short-term bonuses, paid out against clearly established targets, increased the variable part of the compensation, and moved fourteen hundred people into long-term incentive plans, so that key managers became shareholders.

Beyond the management team, too many companies fail to fully harness the talent of their boards, to make the boards more decisive and efficient in helping CEOs do the performance-enhancing job. Value-added boards help coach CEOs, provide real business input and make quick decisions on corporate requests. This first requires just the right composition: board members who really understand the industry and the company they represent, as well as the strengths and weaknesses of the management team. Of course, board members should also be well steeped in the key initiatives and the blueprint, and use its language with management. Indeed, Brabeck elevated Johnson, leader of the GLOBE initiative, to his executive board of managers, which gave the project high visibility among the top managers across the company. The outside board of directors received frequent updates from Johnson himself. Like Nestlé, the best PE investors use boards not to manage the companies they own, but to reinforce the plans and help senior managers make the kinds of rapid and decisive moves that help foster success.

- **Make equity sweat:**  You have to embrace *LBO economics*, which in part means getting comfortable with leverage. As a CEO, you clearly need to have an idea of the amount of cash you need to have on hand for various business needs, such as potential acquisitions. This is a critical distinction as portfolio companies of PE firms can always ask the parent to write a check for needed investment. Having said that, our focus here is on using leverage for cash generation and balance sheet discipline. A higher debt-to-equity ratio helps strengthen managers' focus, ensuring that they view cash as a scarce resource. As English essayist Dr.

Samuel Johnson once observed, "The prospect of being hanged focuses the mind wonderfully." Scarce cash forces managers to aggressively manage working capital and allocate capital expenditures with great discipline. Case in point: in August 2007, Nestlé surprised the market on the heels of stellar earnings by announcing an SF 25 billion stock buyback. Scarce cash also forces managers to work the rest of the balance sheet harder, using it as a dynamic tool for growth rather than a static indicator of performance. This means eliminating unproductive or underperforming capital, often by cutting pieces out of the business. It also may mean finding new ways to convert traditionally fixed assets into sources of financing.

- **Foster a results-oriented mind-set:** The best PE firms also work their magic by helping their portfolio companies foster a *results-oriented mind-set*. Yes, such a mind-set embraces a powerful focus on earnings and cash, driven by the five disciplines just introduced. But it goes much further. It also rests on developing a repeatable formula: repeatable within one activity and also across multiple activities. This repeatability is the key to sustaining results in company after company for smart PE investors. It is a mind-set that rewards an attitude that seeks solutions proactively rather than reacting to events (we call this *being at cause*). It is the opposite of a passive, take no risk, "it happened to us" culture (or *being at effect*). Creating this culture requires both the right managers and the right management processes, as we have discussed. A results mind-set leads to commitment to "resetting the hurdles" to maintain focus. Times change and markets change. The half-life of common wisdom is shorter than ever. Nestlé, for example, has eliminated supervisors right down to the factory floor. "The workers [meet] after [they finish their] shift. They have a special room where they have all their performance data on the wall, and for fifteen to twenty minutes they go through their own performance, and *they* decide what they have to do in order to improve," says Brabeck. "[The fact that] they have to decide counts."[6] As it turns out, when everybody owns the challenge of generating results, very few stones get left unturned, and value is created at all levels.

We use the best private equity practices as the benchmark, but in reality these lessons have been around for a long time. They just haven't been codified as formally by most businesses. Whatever the ownership structure of your company, our advice is to look at how the best PE people operate, and to use their own techniques to compete against them and everybody else.

That is what this memo can help you do.

# Define the Full Potential

The PE game has changed, and here is how.

The way PE funds made money in the 1980s, and for most of the 1990s, was relatively simple. They used networks of contacts to source proprietary deals. Next, they loaded these assets up with debt, sometimes up to 90 percent of the capital structure, thus keeping the equity check needed to buy the business very modest. Over time, as these assets threw off cash, the debt was paid down. Eventually the assets were sold—often for a higher multiple of earnings before interest, taxes, depreciation, and amortization (EBITDA, a measure often used as a proxy for cash flow from operations)—in rising markets. The combination of low entry prices, lots of leverage, and higher exit multiples produced a "perfect storm" of good results: high IRRs and cash-on-cash returns.

For better than a decade, this model was a money machine—but no more. Today, the truly outstanding PE firms have replaced passive stewardship with a hands-on approach to building value in their portfolio companies. Why? Mainly because the engine that generated all those great returns in the past has been sputtering for some time. Almost all properties of more than $100 million in total enterprise value are now sold at auction by aggressive investment banks. The high PE returns of the 1980s attracted an avalanche of new funds—and competition. Today, it is all but impossible to buy assets at a discount to potential value. And we have recently observed that while the debt markets in the 2003–2007 period helped produce spectacular returns by allowing debt multiple levels to increase to amounts not seen since the late 1980s, the future debt cycle will almost assuredly be less friendly than during the past few years.

So at the beginning of this new day in PE, there is really only one way to swim against competitive currents and cyclical market conditions: *creating operating value*. Increasing the cash flow (and hence the value) of acquired companies is the process that the best PE firms are vigorously pursuing to keep generating attractive returns. Shifting gears as soon as a deal is completed, they use a systematic approach to collaborate with management and spot, stage, lead, measure, and profit from strategic and operational improvements.

They get richly rewarded for that systematic approach. Our experience shows that PE deal makers who in the first year of ownership actively plan and launch initiatives using a reliable and repeatable process, earn a cash-on-cash return on their investment that is better than 2.5 times the average industry return.

That fact brings us to the main theme of this section: the starting point for this strong performance begins with *defining the full potential* of the business in question.

How do PE players accomplish this, and how might it translate into a context outside of PE ownership?

## The PE Approach to Defining the Full Potential

The first thing that the best PE firms do is to develop a clear understanding of where and how a business makes money and why they'd want to own it. They conduct a rigorous and dispassionate due diligence, building an objective fact base of the business and its industry. This might be called a "strategic" due diligence, for reasons that will become clear shortly. Typically, they focus on at least five things:[7]

- *Derived demand analysis* (What are the true underlying drivers, how are they changing, and how will they affect demand?)

- *Customer analysis* (What are this business's customers going to do?)

- *Competitive analysis* (What are this business's competitors doing, and how does it stack up against this business?)

- *Environmental analysis* (Are there technological, regulatory, or other issues or trends that may affect future performance positively or negatively?)

- *Microeconomic analysis* (How does this business really make money and where?)

PE firms then set an equity target value for a point in time that is generally three to five years out, based on their due diligence findings, their reading of the full potential of the business and the planned financial structure. The target is based, too, on the assumption that they will be successful at injecting new thinking into the company if required, and that they will be able to partner with management in steering the company toward embracing required changes.

In this era of intense competition, PE firms need to find a reason to pay more than competing strategic and financial buyers. The only compelling reason to pay more than the next bidder is the discovery that the microeconomics of the business can be better than conventional wisdom would imply.

Conversely, the best PE firms are acutely attuned to any red flags that might persuade them to bow out of the process. Like you, PE deal makers are busy; they can't spend their time on low-probability bets. Meanwhile, they are well aware that in most cases, there's someone out there who will overpay for this asset, in part because not everyone is conducting a comparable strategic due diligence. The attitude is, "If someone wants to overpay, fine; it's just not going to be us!"

Top PE buyers never assume that they know everything about the business that they are looking at or the industry it is in. They are also aware that every business and industry is a moving target. So even if they know something about the company or industry at hand, they ask endless questions. (Advance knowledge can certainly lead to sharper questions at the outset, but there is always plenty of homework still to be done.) They live by the motto "In God we trust. All others bring data."

Good investors put little faith in the offering books that are put together for companies that are on the block. These books are compiled mainly based on market research reports and analysts' reports, which in turn are largely informed by off-the-shelf data. For example, these books rarely look deeply into the demand drivers that industry growth will depend on in the future. Those preparing them usually just take historical growth rates and tweak them a bit using management estimates of future growth and the readily available market research reports. Obviously, market research reports can be, and often are, wrong. It certainly makes no sense to double-check offering books with the same sources used by the bankers who put them together in the first place!

Instead, the best PE buyers do their own homework. They and their advisers drill deeply into the key drivers of demand and how they might behave in the future. They interview the key decision makers in the customer base, making sure they cover a majority of the target company's revenues. They approach suppliers the same way, looking at costs. They always analyze the competition (where possible, they interview competitors) and dig out information relating to their strategy, operations, cost position, technological sophistication, financial situation, and so on.

What are smart buyers looking for? They are looking to determine what the full potential of the business is and what it could be worth in three to five years. This becomes their target equity value. At the same time, they are looking to identify the few key initiatives that should be emphasized to reach that full potential. Planning to do a dozen things simultaneously usually turns into a recipe for disappointment. Instead, the PE buyer focuses on three to five critical initiatives—and also makes it clear what the company is *not* going to do. This process helps ensure the business does not waste time, money, and management bandwidth on the wrong issues. In our experience, the discipline of *not* doing things can preserve tremendous value. Therefore, identifying the full potential path early is critical.

Of paramount interest to most PE buyers is the *time frame* to reach full potential. While the key initiatives on their short list typically range from immediate to longer-term impact, many PE buyers adopt a three- to five-year time horizon for their full potential plan to materialize—which corresponds with their average anticipated length of overall investment in the company. There are PE players whose time frame is somewhat longer; these players may well invest in even longer-term initiatives. And as CEOs like Peter Brabeck will point out quite graphically, the returns available to companies purposed to sustain a business—for example, to breed and raise cows and sustain a dairy for the long term—will be different from those aimed to acquire and resell—to buy a few cows, milk them hard, and send them to the slaughterhouse.

But smart PE owners, too, must think about sustainability. Because they will be selling the business to another buyer at some point, they need to ensure that the company they have invested in has a sustainable wealth creation platform. Without it, the next set of owners doing their strategic due diligence (be they private owners or public markets) will likely sniff out future value deterioration, which could devastate the seller's returns.

So, three to five years might be the starting point (and the point at which most things are reasonably actionable for most companies), but it is by no means the end point.

There are examples of companies in both the United States and Europe that are on their fourth or fifth successive private equity owner—with each owner making good returns upon exit. Take, for example, French plumbing supply group Frans Bonhomme SA, which has been bought and sold four times in eleven years—each time for a profit. In such cases, the next PE firm often continues implementing what the previous one started, making substantial changes only if they think they can add further value. True, PE firms sell. But they *must* sell because they have to repatriate capital to their limited partners—that is part of their business model. It has nothing to do with the validity of the portfolio company business model they've created. In fact, the nice thing about PE firms cashing out is that it shows us how they did in a very tangible way.

## For Example?

One case in point involves the Sealy Corporation, the mattress maker that was purchased in 1997 by an investment group led by Bain Capital and Charlesbank Capital Partners.[8] Together with Sealy's management, the two PE firms assembled a team to launch an appraisal of the company's competitive position, prioritize opportunities to improve performance, and develop a detailed road map to guide implementation. The team probed every corner of Sealy's business and challenged every assumption. This involved reviewing Sealy's growth record and underlying trends; analyzing its cost structure and drivers of increasing costs; closely examining competitors' performance and products; interviewing and segmenting both customers (retail) and consumers; and for each segment, determining its product and service requirements.

What did they discover under the mattress? A lot of unexpected, actionable facts:

- Sealy had a cost disadvantage, and its sales mix had shifted toward the less profitable portions of its product line. As a result, Sealy's profit margin was declining while its main competitors' margins were improving.

- Although the complexity of Sealy's product line was increasing, this was not the primary driver of the company's cost problem. While complexity generated some additional costs, product differentiation was critical to support high retail and manufacturer margins.

- Retail floor space for selling mattresses was highly constrained, and the best opportunity to boost profits lay in trading up slots to higher price points.

- Sealy had a particularly low share in smaller accounts. Yet this segment offered higher margins and faster growth than Sealy's typical customers. This was a pleasant surprise as management had not fully appreciated the profitability of higher-end, mom-and-pop stores and therefore had not honed an operating model for cost-effectively serving them.

As a result of this rigorous assessment of Sealy's true full potential, the two PE firms set a value-creation target of five times their equity investment. To reach that target, they zeroed in on a few crucial initiatives.

One of the key initiatives was a complete redesign of Sealy's core Posturepedic mattress line. Critically,

Sealy shifted away from a costly, two-sided design that allowed mattress owners to do something most didn't bother to: flip their mattresses. Instead, Sealy designed a new and improved "no flip" mattress whose technology improved Sealy's margins and leapfrogged the technology of its chief rival, Simmons, which had been selling a one-sided mattress for years. Three other major initiatives that sprang from Sealy's full-potential assessment involved account planning strategies and tools, pricing, and manufacturing changes to reduce material yield loss.

This rigorous assessment also revealed what Sealy should not do. For example, before the sale, Sealy's management team had mapped out a plan to increase revenues by its volume of mid-priced mattresses. A detailed product profitability analysis convinced Sealy management that concentrating on higher price points would raise profitability and reward its retailers most. This was accomplished in two ways: by focusing the redesign of Sealy's core mattress line on the targeted price points; and by developing decision-making tools that would assist sales reps in maximizing the profitability of each account's merchandising mix.

The key growth and cost-cutting initiatives increased EBITDA by more than 50 percent over three years.

Defining the company's full potential, including a target value and a short list of key initiatives, is only the preamble to the down-in-the-trenches activities that come in the blueprint-development phase (as described in the next section). But before we leave our Sealy case study behind, it is worth fast-forwarding to reveal how the story turned out. In 2004, Sealy's owners sold the company to Kohlberg Kravis Roberts & Company (KKR), netting a better than fivefold return on equity. KKR willingly paid this price because of the strength of the full-potential plan and clear momentum in results already banked. Under KKR ownership, Sealy continued to grow EBITDA and reap the benefits of the full-potential program.

## *Your* Approach to Defining the Company's Full Potential

How does this full-potential exercise apply to a public or private company?

Obviously, to the extent that you are in the acquisitions game, you would benefit from being among the best-informed bidders at the table. But our focus here is broader. We argue that corporations can benefit from a rigorous, PE-style process of internal due diligence, aimed at building an objective fact base about the company and at discovering its full potential. We argue, too, that such a process of "rediscovery," conducted on a regular basis, can be absolutely critical to your company's health.

Step out of the twelve-to-eighteen-month budget planning cycle and ask, How high is up? What is the company really worth? Step out of the twelve-month or twenty-four-month payback cycles and ask, Which handful of key initiatives, either undertaken from scratch or reinvigorated, will have enormous impact three to five years down the road?

Think "blank sheet of paper." Why would somebody want to own this business or its component parts? What can this business become?

Unfortunately, your current management accounting system is unlikely to spit out good answers for you. We would go as far as observing that many corporate management teams know far less about the environment in which they operate than they think they do. As a result, they often don't challenge their own conventional wisdom until it is obvious what needs to be done—in other words, *too late*.

Instead, you have to start by emulating the PE buyers' due diligence to define your company's full potential and dig out the facts bottom up. You must collect facts on the key drivers of demand and how they are likely to behave in the future. You must interview customers to understand how they make purchase decisions and how your key products or services stack up against those of the competition. Are there gaps in performance that need to be addressed? Where and how? What are the customers' future purchase intentions if we do nothing? How will that affect our market share? If we change things, what is the upside? What are the risks? How has pricing changed over time for key products and services? What are customers demanding and competitors doing that will affect the future pricing environment? Are my costs truly competitive? How can we conduct an apples-to-apples cost comparison versus key competition to understand how much and where we are advantaged or disadvantaged? What can we do to close any gaps? What can we do to leapfrog competitors? Will regulations or technology change in some fashion that will impact the business? How and how much? Do we understand where and how we really make money? Do we have unprofitable products? Do we make money on all of our customers?

All of these questions are hard to answer. For many of them, you can find hard data (customers and costs, some parts of derived demand) if you know where to look and know how to put it together to define a future environment for the company. For others, like macroeconomic cycles and technology changes, there will be ranges of outcomes that need to be evaluated. The bottom line is, you need to see what the facts say about the company and its environment and what levers can actually be pulled to create value, if you want to really define the full potential of a business. You also need to fully understand the investments and risks facing the business in the future to complete the picture.

The story of the acquisition in the late 1990s of a fishing company called American Seafoods by the private equity firm Centre Partners is a good example of a comprehensive due diligence effort that looked for risks and uncovered unexpected good news.[9]

At the time, the company, which caught and processed Alaskan pollack and other species from seven fishing trawlers operating in the U.S. Bering Sea, was owned by a Norwegian parent company. But when the U.S. Congress enacted a law that made it illegal for a foreign concern to own companies fishing in American waters, the Norwegian parent was forced to sell. Although American Seafoods had experienced a jump in profits in 1999—more than doubling the three preceding years' average EBITDA—the fishing business did not, at first blush, seem particularly attractive. Historically subject to wide swings in supplies and prices, and under increasingly tight regulation, it seemed fated to volatile and potentially weak returns.

Was this fishing business as unattractive as conventional wisdom would imply? Would a buyer be paying too much at even a modest cash flow multiple? Centre Partners sent in a crack due diligence team, combining experts in consumer products, fishing operations, and marine biology, and found that, far from being a blip, American Seafoods' profit boom had the potential to expand.

It was a global analysis of the health of major fisheries and of the derived demand for Alaskan pollack that turned up the most interesting data. The team discovered that the total biomass of the U.S. Alaskan pollack fishery was expected to grow in coming years, while the biomasses of competing fisheries—Russian pollack and Atlantic cod, most notably—were dropping, often at a fast clip. Global supplies of pollack and cod would likely fall, but the share of the market represented by U.S. Alaskan pollack would increase. That was good news from a revenue and pricing standpoint, and the news got even better when the due diligence team looked more closely at trends in fish prices. Although pollack prices had recently increased, as overall supplies fell, they remained well below the levels of competing whitefish like cod, tilapia, and hoki. As a result, there seemed little chance that pollack would be subject to significant price competition for the foreseeable future. The big

Japanese market for pollack roe, meanwhile, remained strong while supplies were falling, leading to a sharp and sustainable increase in roe prices that seemed likely to benefit American Seafoods well into the future.

The last piece of good news was that the number of ships allowed to fish Alaskan waters for pollack was tightly regulated and would not be increasing. Thus, American Seafoods had a fleet of boats with stable competition in a geography that had a growing pollack biomass in the face of increasing demand. Centre Partners was able to calculate the profitability and return on invested capital on a ship-by-ship basis with a high level of confidence. Suddenly, the fishing business seemed very attractive indeed.

Because of the results of the due diligence analysis, Centre Partners made a successful bid for American Seafoods. It turned out to be quite a catch. Within three years, EBITDA nearly doubled again, and the private equity firm had recapitalized the company and sold a portion of its stake. In the process, Centre Partners realized nearly four times its initial investment and retained control of the business as it sought to further grow revenue and increase profits. In 2006, Centre Partners sold its remaining stake to the company's management group and Coastal Villages Region Fund, the company's Alaskan business partner.

## Using the Fact Base

Use the fact base to define the full potential of your business. This means a couple of things. First, determine what your company could be worth three to five years down the road, and make it the overarching goal of your management team.

Second, identify the crucial few initiatives that will get you there. Challenge "business as usual," and think along multiple dimensions:

- Incremental moves that will make our current activities more profitable

- Bold departures that will reposition some or all of our activities for future success

- Shifting of resources away from those activities that don't represent the future of the company

You might be thinking, we already have a five-year strategy plan. Indeed, most companies have one. But on closer examination, too often those plans boil down to overly simple and underambitious goals. Why? One reason is that most corporations aren't good at making tough choices. In strategic plans, too many public companies are inclined to make the assumption that most divisions and product lines will grow at their historical rate. They are *not* inclined to think hard about which division might be divested to allow a "double-down" on a more promising sister division.

By the same token, too many are disinclined to bet heavily on new initiatives. The failure of any such new initiative would be highly visible and could be destructive to senior corporate careers. Even a delayed success could be damaging, given Wall Street's short-term focus.

## The Bottom Line

While strategic due diligence may sound daunting, it need not be. If the derived demand, customer, competitive, environmental and microeconomic analyses are not standard operating procedure for your company—especially at the level of detail described in the preceding pages—consider getting outside help to guide you through them the first time and help you institutionalize them. Along the way, make sure that you and your helpers *focus on the actionable*. Remember: you are zeroing in on the three to five initiatives. Do not let your organization get lost in the clouds! And to the extent possible, run an ongoing culture check. Who is excited about this process, and who is not? The status quo is immensely powerful, in most organizations. You will need to find strong allies who can help you through the longer-term process of creating value.

Last, you might be interested to know that some of the best PE firms do *exactly the same thing* after they've held a particular property for some time. No, they're obviously not going to "buy it again." Rather, they want to look at the business anew, with an eye toward a recast and improved value proposition. Leading companies should do the same.

## Monday Morning Matters: Define the Full Potential

Conduct due diligence on yourself: think in terms of "strategic due diligence," and take an outside-in view of:

- Derived demand analysis

- Customer analysis

- Competitive analysis

- Environmental analysis

- Microeconomic analysis

Specifically define the full potential for a business: how high can cash flow grow?

Embrace bold moves and big changes, if such changes are required to achieve full potential.

Identify the three to five core initiatives, and specify what not to do.

Adopt a medium-term focus (three to five years).

Do a culture check: where is the momentum of the status quo coming from?

Act fast to do your due diligence—this is a priority.

Do it again two to three years from now.

---

# Develop
# the Blueprint

At the end of strategic due diligence to assess a company's full potential, as described in the previous section, the PE buyer has a good sense of "how high is up" and what few core initiatives will lead the way there.

Let's assume that you have conducted a strategic due diligence on your own company. As a result, you now have a clear sense of your organization's capabilities and potential. Like the PE buyer, you have identified a short list of the highest-potential initiatives in the company—the areas that deserve systematic investments and attention in the near and middle term, to ensure the highest possible return within three to five years.

Now the goal is to make that *real*. This is accomplished through the development of a blueprint.

## How PE Firms Develop a Blueprint

In the blueprint phase, PE buyers start with two key sets of data points:

- The three- to five-year full-potential equity value.

- The few big initiatives (again, usually somewhere between three and five, rarely more than a half dozen) that the management team and PE firm have decided to embrace aggressively in their full-potential analysis.

The blueprint brings the initiatives to life. Substantial initiatives need to be matched to the reality of resource constraints. To achieve a goal, certain activities will be required. Investments, too, will be required. People will be needed to perform these activities in a certain sequence and by a certain deadline. A blueprint is a strategic operating plan that lays out in pragmatic detail how an organization will successfully complete its initiatives and thereby achieve full potential.

For each initiative, the blueprint works its way down to a very detailed road map for action. The initiative gets actions, resources, timelines, milestones, metrics, and deliverables attached to it. To the extent that the unfolding initiatives are interrelated, those interrelationships (and any critical-path issues) are also spelled out in the blueprint.

Just to underscore this key point: the PE's blueprint is *very different* from the traditional company's strategic planning binders, which often tend to focus on "what we want to be" at the expense of "how we are going to deliver." The PE's blueprint is only about *action*. It is about executing on the initiatives and how one dollar becomes several dollars within a specific time period.

To illustrate, let's come back to the Sealy example. One of Sealy's key initiatives involved the redesign of its core mattress, based on a common platform, to drive growth, improve manufacturability, and reduce costs. The team devised a detailed blueprint that involved a number of specific actions, including analyzing retailers' preferences and competitors' offerings to determine ideal product attributes; costing out alternative platform designs with R&D and manufacturing; laying out a product development timeline, process requirements, and management roles as part of a cross-functional product development program office; identifying required manufacturing investments, training, and ramp-up; and coordinating the rollout of brands to different retailers and across different product lines (in other words, which brands got the new design and which retailers got it first).

Sealy's blueprint rigor paid off. The new mattress design was rolled out on schedule. It limited capital expenditures, improved EBITDA by 22 percent, and maximized reinvestment in the premium price points targeted.

## The Corporate Equivalent of Developing a Blueprint

In the previous section, we talked about how difficult it is for most corporations to make tough choices and bet on new initiatives. In the blueprint phase, you need to be getting beyond those limitations. You need to be committed to your short list of key initiatives and to designing action-oriented road maps to implement them.

Start by having your own notion of what the blueprint should look like. Then bring your senior management team together for an intensive, inclusive planning process in the figurative "windowless room"—for however long it takes. Bring in an outside facilitator to run the process, if you think that will foster (1) collaboration and (2) forward momentum. Ask: what resources (money and people) will be required, and where will they come from?

Work the facts hard. Challenge the champions of the status quo. Use the process to get the full management team well versed in and in agreement with both the fact base and the blueprint. When Michael Capellas took over at Compaq in 1999, the company was troubled by infighting. He put the entire management team together in a room to agree on the turnaround blueprint. Three days later, they all marched out of that room together, unified.[10] The plan not only helped the company turn around but also helped fetch a $20 billion price from Hewlett-Packard.

## Developing a Blueprint at Korea First

As a case in point, consider how Newbridge Capital—a partnership between private equity luminaries TPG and Blum Capital Partners—used a blueprint process to help transform Korea First Bank from a bankrupt industrial creditor into a world-class financial institution.[11]

Before the Asian economic crisis in 1997, Korea First had been the country's number-one corporate bank. It was heavily damaged during the crisis. As a result, when Newbridge assumed control of Korea First from government receivership in 2000, the bank was saddled with a costly institutional branch network, built with dedicated space for back-office processes. Newbridge set about assessing how the bank could reach its full potential, and uncovered one overarching opportunity: to transform Korea First into a competitive retail bank. According to due diligence, getting there would take three critical initiatives:

- Korea First would need to shift its bank branch structure to serve retail customers.

- It would need to develop the back-office support and customer service capabilities that a competitive retail bank would need, which would require upgrading its IT system and aligning it to the new business goals.

- Finally, the bank would need to create a different kind of sales force, one focused on customer service and retail sales.

Then, Newbridge and Korea First's management team carefully choreographed a plan—the blueprint—that detailed the groundwork required to accomplish the key initiatives.

The goal of the first initiative was to reconfigure and simplify Korea First's branches in high-traffic consumer locations. Rather than divert resources to rebuilding branches from scratch, Newbridge worked with managers and redesigned the existing infrastructure. The team consolidated corporate business into a handful of large-scale branches. They closed some locations, shrinking the branch network by thirty-one offices, and then reconfigured the remaining ones, removing back-office functions and focusing them instead on reaching out to consumers through customer sales. The simplification resulted in $50 million of bottom-line improvements within a year.

For the second initiative, the new owners assigned a high-level executive team—supported by outside technical experts—to spearhead a change management program to consolidate loan processing, credit collection, and trade finance into two new customer service centers. This initiative included a parallel step that dedicated project teams to upgrade Korea First's IT organization, adding telemarketing and customer call-center capacities. By choreographing these steps in parallel, Newbridge was able to make Korea First's new facilities operational within five months.

Finally, the blueprint took into account the need to build the right organization with the right salespeople to support the full-potential plan. As in many Asian business cultures, Korea's labor and management have a loyalty compact supported by strong employment laws. The turmoil of Korea First's bankruptcy and sale left the bank with a demoralized

frontline workforce and an imperative to retain employees in the transition. Recognizing this, management tapped key human resource staffers as allies in
the change campaign, making them more available
to branch-office workers. Management broadcast the
bank's commitment to retain employees who were
made redundant by downsizing, helping to train
those workers for new positions in customer service
and sales. In all, branch closings and work-process
changes ended up claiming eight hundred jobs, but
these were more than offset by newly created positions that displaced workers could apply for. The
candor and support—reinforced by cash incentives
for working more efficiently—helped Korea First
shift its business quickly to the consumer side and
improve its efficiency, cutting loan approval time by
75 percent.

By 2005, five years after Newbridge's acquisition,
the bank's new infrastructure for loan processing and
call support was best-in-class, and Korea First again
became number one, this time in growing sales of
retail mortgages: with one of the industry's lowest
ratios of nonperforming loans, its balance sheet was
the nation's strongest. The improved infrastructure
not only paved the way to speedier service but also
lowered cost: the average number of staff per retail
branch dropped from ten to eight. The payoff: in Jan-

uary 2005, the British banking group Standard Chartered bought Korea First for $3.25 billion, a nearly fourfold return on the private equity fund's equity investment. Since then, Standard Chartered has replicated Korea First's model in other countries.

## Getting Started

Your own corporate starting point determines how easy it will be for you to embrace the blueprint process. Some companies—certainly GE of Jack Welch's day and Nestlé under Peter Brabeck—are highly skilled at the fundamentals of developing a blueprint.

Unfortunately, they are the exceptions to the rule.

As we said at the end of the previous section, if any aspect of this blueprint process sounds daunting or foreign to you, *get help*. Plan on budgeting between two and six months for the blueprint process, on average, with an eye toward launching your first initiative within the first one hundred days. Some blueprints will take longer than others because they must take into account more complexity than others given the nature and competitive context of a given business. Be aware, though, that because the full-potential thesis development process cycles every few years, the blueprint will, to some extent, always be a work in progress. Whatever your refreshment cycle, this will lead to new thinking about the blueprint. You may also conclude that with your first few initiatives well underway, you can afford to go to your "B" list for a second round of investments—the ones that just missed being on the critical list the first time around.

Perhaps you're wondering whether the "activist" PE firms have an advantage that you *don't* have: a shared sense across the organization that the mold is being broken and that a newer, more effective business operating model is possible. After all, aren't PE owners known for their single-mindedness? Doesn't the very act of investment by a PE firm or consortium in a given company create in that company a sense of urgency, anxiety, and expectation—an environment that, for better or worse, tends to foster change versus the status quo?

The answer to this last question is *yes*, but there is really no reason why you, as the CEO, can't create a change-oriented atmosphere. Developing a blueprint can help CEOs draw a bright starting line. This is especially true for new corporate CEOs, who in fact face many of the same challenges as PE decision makers. Even when they are promoted from within, new CEOs have to win over skeptics quickly and start breaking the mold. Launching a strategic due diligence to define full potential within the first hundred days can help new CEOs light a controlled fire under the organization, cement relationships with other key executives and the board, spot talent deep within the organization, and mobilize the company around a common vision.

But doing the due diligence and developing a blueprint can help any business leader who concludes that his or her company is falling behind its competition along some critical dimension, or who is truly looking to better his company's old standards of performance. Once you discover an improved path, start down it immediately. Every day you wait enhances your competitors' opportunity and/or diminishes yours. If you have concluded that your organization needs a restart, you too can use a blueprint to good effect.

## Monday Morning Matters: Develop the Blueprint

Develop a road map for your three to five *key initiatives*, and *focus*.

Start macro, and work down to what you will do differently on "Monday morning, 8 a.m."—that is, the *actionable* to-do list.

Be specific and pragmatic.

Let the *facts* win the day.

Create excitement and alignment.

Budget two to six months (at least the first time).

---

# Accelerate Performance

How do you build a house? You start with a vision, and then you develop a blueprint that captures that vision down to the specifics: everything from the wiring to the doorknobs. But even at the end of the blueprint process, you're still a long way from a finished and functioning house!

In this section, we look at how the best PE firms "build the house" through a process of *accelerating performance*. This process is a combination of many separate activities that influence and reinforce each other. It involves molding the organization to the blueprint and monitoring its success. It involves setting up mechanisms to move the blueprint forward and to motivate and reward the key players.

## How PE Firms Accelerate Performance

The first priority, when PE players set out to turn a blueprint into a reality, is to *mold the organization around the blueprint.* They partner with management and help to identify the levels within the company where help is likely to be needed, and then they make sure that help can be found at that level. Thus, they avoid potential mismatches between the blueprint and managerial capacity.

If necessary, these PE firms also work with management down to one more level of specificity: *which* bodies in *which* seats? Which internal talents are a promising fit with this particular initiative? And what external talent can be brought to bear, including via outsourcing? Make no mistake: PE firms for the most part don't run companies. They don't *want* to run them, and will be the first to tell you that they wouldn't do a very good job if they did run them. The best PE firms simply want to ensure that management is positioned for success. They are there, with internal or external resources, to help management deliver on its blueprint.

The best PE firms foster senior management accountability. They do so in a number of ways, including insisting on executive sponsorship of individual initiatives. Each initiative gets an "owner"—someone who has a direct personal stake in its success. They also make the blueprint the centerpiece of their senior management dialogue. This means, among other things, monthly in-depth reviews of progress and results. In addition, they tie their executives' compensation (including the equity portion) to the results of the executives' own units and initiatives, effectively making them owners. Often, management teams own 10 to 30 percent of the total equity in their businesses, through grants, direct investment (if necessary, borrowings from the PE firm) and rewards for hitting blueprint targets. Not only do they "think like owners," they *are* owners.

The best PE players also embrace program management tools to drive implementation. One of the key tools often used is the program office, which governs the blueprint and ensures that each initiative delivers value on time. The program office is not extra bandwidth. It is a structure composed of a subset of cross-functional folks from across the organization—some senior, some junior. The program office reports to senior management every couple of weeks to ensure that things are on track and to highlight any problems or key decisions that need to be made. The program office also pays close attention to issues that cut across functions, and resolves "territorial" disputes. In addition, the program office, along with senior management, plays a key role in making sure that the tough and often unpopular decisions get made and that people accept accountability. Not every blueprint requires a program office. However, the bolder the initiatives and the more change they create, the more likely that a program office will be helpful, if not required.

Finally, the best PE players have learned to track the key measures of success for the initiatives that will ultimately create equity value versus just relying on the standard array of management accounting data.

## Watching the Vital Few Metrics

At the risk of stating the obvious: PE firms obsessively watch key metrics, including market data and performance data.

PE buyers get paid when their bets pay off. They therefore keep a finger on the pulse of each portfolio company, seeking reassurance that things are going according to the plan, that the timetable can be met, and that the payoff will be there.

What may *not* be so obvious, however, is that not all PE firms track the same things. Some stop with the fundamentals of markets and financial results. Others—the more activist buyers—dig deeper. They track metrics that help them monitor progress toward operational goals before it shows up in the financial results. Rather than waiting to find out if the map (i.e., the blueprint) got them to the right place, activist investors use their onboard navigational systems constantly to make sure that they are headed in the right direction.

Thus PE firms focus on *operational* measures that look forward, point to root causes, and thereby spur action. Measuring "profit per customer," for example, looks backward. Measuring the "number of high-value customers acquired last month," by contrast, illuminates a meaningful trend. Similarly, a measure of "declining sales" certainly points to a problem, but "revenue churn"—specifically, how many customers canceled contracts—tells management where to intervene.

For example, at Crown Castle, executives track one operational measure religiously, above all others: the "lease-up" rate, or the number of antennas per tower. A trend toward more antennas has to be a good thing; a trend toward fewer antennas has to be a bad thing. This is the operational measure that most clearly reveals Crown Castle's progress in increasing its value.

PE firms watch *cash* more closely than earnings, knowing that cash remains a true barometer of financial performance, as earnings are subject to distortion. As a rule, they prefer to calculate return on invested capital, which indicates the actual return on the money put into a business rather than fuzzier measures like return on accounting capital employed.

For example, a PE firm with a portfolio company involved in wine making used cash flow and its cash-conversion cycle, not return on assets or economic value added. This is because wine making is a very asset-intensive business with some peculiar characteristics. Using metrics that pull depreciation and amortization out of earnings penalized the company for hanging on to vineyards and cellars of aging wine, which actually were increasing in value over time.

The primary financial measure Crown Castle focuses on is cash flow per share versus an absolute measure such as pure cash flow (which can be increased by acquisition, but not necessarily enhance cash flow per share). This ensures the company is focusing its efforts on growth strategies that increase shareholder value and not growth for growth's sake. In addition to being Crown Castle's primary financial measure, it is also the measure the company reinforces with Wall Street analysts.

Managers in the best PE firms are careful to avoid imposing one set of measures across their entire portfolios, preferring to tailor measures to each business in the portfolio. "We use *their* metrics, not our metrics," explains James Coulter, founding partner of TPG. "You have to use performance measures that make sense for the business unit itself, rather than some preconceived notion from the corporate center."[12] Finally, as mentioned before, PE firms reward their managers for hitting blueprint targets by tying compensation to the key metrics.

## Getting the Metrics Right

Let's look at a case in point that hinges on the challenge of defining the right metrics. As you'll see, choosing what to monitor is highly dependent on the specifics of the situation at hand.

Settling on the right numbers to pursue was a cornerstone of the strategy developed by CVC Asia Pacific and CCMP Capital Asia (formerly JPMorgan Partners Asia) to turn around Singapore Yellow Pages (SYP). The two firms led a consortium that purchased the telephone directory publisher from SingTel, the local telecommunications company, in June 2003.

The first order of business for the new owners: creating a sense of urgency in an organization that had grown complacent and stale. Despite an 87 percent market share and no serious rival to challenge its dominance, SYP saw its revenues slide by 40 percent between 1999 and 2003, while profit margins deteriorated. Advertisers were defecting—and so, too, was SYP's sales force, with the annual turnover rate among the demoralized sales reps topping 50 percent.

The new owners and SYP management developed an initiative that called for a major overhaul of advertising sales. The blueprint set concrete revenue and profit growth targets for each of a dozen clusters of high-priority customers, ranked by potential value. It revamped the sales prospecting process, replacing the overlapping, uncoordinated efforts of telephone customer service reps and individual account managers with a process in which sales teams set priorities by determining advertisers' current and potential value to the company. To keep the sales team focused, management ratcheted up the number of accounts each sales rep served, and established guidelines for the number of calls or visits needed to close a sale. They benchmarked the company's sales and marketing performance against the industry's best practices, and established a new incentive-heavy compensation scheme that delivered significant rewards to top performers.

The specific metrics used were tailored to customer segments: retention rates and the amount of up-selling of ads to "platinum" customers, cross-selling of multiple products to "gold" customers, and the number of new account sign-ups and penetration by industry vertical in the "bronze" customer category. Additionally, the measurement of performance via quantitative metrics (such as return on investment, or ROI) gave the sales force a new communication tool with their clients. The sales force found that renewal rates were higher in categories where they could articulate a high ROI from the client's ad expenditure.

The new performance metrics also provided a regular report card on whether the SYP turnaround was on track. They made transparent for the first time how much revenue per customer each dollar invested in the sales effort yielded. The clear metrics helped give a powerful signal to other potential investors that the new sales force strategy was working.

A little more than a year after making the acquisition, the private equity partners floated an initial public offering of SYP shares, locking in a gain of 2.6 times their original investment while still retaining a 20 percent stake in the company.

## What Accelerating Performance Means to You

In a general sense, most corporations are attuned to the need to get the right people in the right seats and to get people to own the organization's key initiatives.

But most organizations aren't good at delivering against these needs, and therefore fail to accelerate performance in the way the best PE investors do. In one candid conversation, a CEO told us that he not only didn't have the managers that he needed to undertake the actions that his blueprint had mapped out; he also didn't have the talent needed in HR to *hire* the missing managers!

This is a more common problem than one might suppose. Ask yourself, again, what is needed to make the agreed-on blueprint *real*. Translate the specific actions of the blueprint into the responsibility of specific individuals. Who, *exactly*, is on the hook for this specific outcome? Where are the talent deficits, and how are you going to overcome them? And even if you have plenty of talent, how do you guarantee that your people are organized in a way that decisions—the coin of the realm—get made and acted on wisely and swiftly?

We often help companies think through what we call a "RAPID" scenario for decision making: in other words, just who is responsible for *recommending* an action (the R), *agreeing* (A), providing *input* (I), *deciding* (D), and ultimately *performing* (P), or executing against the decision.[13] Think of it as decision-making software, shared across the organization. If you can effectively rewrite the software of decision making, you can effect significant change while still steering clear of the grand reorganization. Reorganizations are toxic, by and large because they tend to be time-consuming and intensely political. And, too often, the new structure is divorced from the very initiatives that lead to full potential.

Next, figure out the close-to-the-ground measures that you're going to monitor, in order to make sure that you know about your company's performance before it shows up in the financials. Don't let your company default to the kind of numbers that your enterprise resource planning (ERP) system is likely to grind out. Instead, look for data that will help you understand whether a specific initiative is succeeding according to the most relevant metrics. Is that data cash based, market based, competition based, or operationally based? If you can't get it with your current resources, what do you have to add?

At Nestlé, Peter Brabeck put very specific measures against each of the four critical initiatives in his full-potential scenario. In the case of "innovation and renovation" of his product portfolio, where his blueprint called for retooling his research and development functions, the target was clear: new products should account for 20 percent of the company's portfolio each year, and all products needed to score a minimum 60-40 preference among relevant consumers versus competitor products, and offer a better nutritional profile. The ultimate measure would be organic growth, aimed at 5 to 6 percent per year with ever-improving margins. The specificity of these measures allowed Nestlé to affirm that its change program remained on track and to rally employees and investors around concrete milestones.

You and your senior colleagues will want to think about the kinds of program management mechanisms you might adopt—for example, the program office mentioned earlier—that could take forward the blueprint and ensure it is on track to deliver.

Several years ago we helped the new CEO of a large, public European industrial business set up a program office. He had been handed the keys to a company that was essentially insolvent. In fact, the company had earned its cost of capital just once in the previous thirteen years and had borrowed money from banks to continue paying a dividend! The share price had collapsed to the equivalent of pennies. Analysts were not excited, as the company participated in a variety of unrelated businesses that served customers as diverse as steel kiln manufacturers and railroad car makers. We dug in with the new CEO and helped him define the full potential, which was set at ten times the current equity value (obviously we were starting with a very small number), and set the initiatives, which included consolidating and selling certain divisions, reinvigorating organic growth in others, managing pricing more effectively, dramatically reducing general and administrative (G&A) expense, and squeezing the assets to make the organization more capital efficient.

Clearly, such far-reaching change required a program office to track the transformation. The program office was staffed with key executives such as the COO, corporate controller, vice president of R&D, vice president of manufacturing and engineering, and head of HR. We helped install the physical tools, such as reporting templates and simple spreadsheets, to track the initiatives. This group met weekly initially and then biweekly to ensure that the blueprint was being followed and that key milestones were being met. If they weren't met, then changes were made internally to find people who could meet the targets. The program office stayed in existence (while undergoing changes over time) for several years. When the transformation was complete, the company had reduced its divisions from nine to four, had slashed corporate G&A by 70 percent, and had recorded several quarters of record organic growth. The company hit its aggressive ten times increase in value in just three years. This example is admittedly extreme, but a good program office can be invaluable in providing a consistent helping hand to senior managers while ensuring that the initiatives to achieve full potential remain on track.

## Thinking About Compensation

Let's conclude this section with a brief look at compensation issues. Earlier, in the PE context, we introduced the idea of tying rewards and compensation to performance and thereby creating an intense sense of ownership among the company's key leaders. Obviously, if you're the head of a publicly traded company, there are limits on the ways that you can use equity as an incentive. Even the time-honored tool of the stock option has its limits—and may be subjected to additional limits in the near future.

There's nothing to prevent you, however, from using bonuses—*substantial* bonuses—to reward outstanding performance within a key initiative. The simple screen to put all such bonuses through is whether the additional compensation is directly linked to an outcome that was within the individual's control. Too many corporations tie incentives to the bottom line, which isn't easily moved by an individual or working group within the organization. As a result they waste money intended to focus motivation.

You may well hear grumblings about these substantial bonuses being reserved for people who are working on the favored initiatives. Most likely, you can point to other examples in your company's history where special bonus pools were created for people working on specific critical tasks. (The members of merger integration teams, for example, often receive bonuses equal to 100 percent of their salaries—in part because if they do their jobs well, they may work themselves out of a job.) Point to those examples if and when the grumblings arise. Point out, once again, that these initiatives are critical to the success of the company.

And point out that the success of these initiatives is likely to lead to more initiatives and a broader base of involvement, including fast and surprising promotions that help careers take off. Indeed, Chris Johnson was handpicked by Brabeck to run the GLOBE initiative as a younger executive with an impressive track record in sales and marketing, having implemented innovative programs in Japan, France, Taiwan, and the United States. On the heels of GLOBE's success, which Brabeck credits with helping Nestlé garner two years of back-to-back organic growth at or close to 6 percent, Brabeck promoted Johnson to deputy executive vice president of information systems, logistics, and GLOBE. "The best promotion I can give him," Brabeck told a CNN reporter, "is recognition for what he has been doing on this project."[14]

## Monday Morning Matters:
## Accelerate Performance

Mold the organization around the blueprint.

Match talent to key initiatives.

Make someone *own* each activity.

Adopt program management tools—for example, a program office.

Monitor what really matters:

- Operational indicators

- Cash, not earnings

- The critical few metrics

Use metrics to *stay ahead of* financial results.

Use rewards to motivate and align—that is, pay employees for what you want them to do.

# Harness the Talent

How do the best PE players achieve their spectacular returns? One part of the answer lies in their ability to *harness talent*. As we've noted in the previous section, this means people up and down the chain of command, but particularly in frontline positions in the key-initiative areas. It means linking rewards with performance—a subject introduced in the previous section, which we'll delve into more deeply here.

It also means building and using the board of directors. PE owners give the boards of directors of their portfolio companies much running room. In fact, by bringing their special talents to bear, those boards often play an absolutely critical role in the success of their companies.

## How PE Firms Harness Talent

PE players are absolutely unbending in their insistence on *performance*. It's not that they're cold-blooded, or heartless, or inhumane. It's just that their three-to-five-year time horizon doesn't allow for very many misfires. They are systematic about thinking through what they need, what they've got, and where they need to fill the breach. This doesn't leave much room for turning a blind eye to missed performance goals. Even though it is always hard to move people without disrupting the team, PE players bite the bullet. They act quickly to replace senior managers who fail to deliver or who are judged inadequate to the challenge.

Where do PE firms find the right executive talent? As a rule, they conduct a broad search, looking well beyond the scope of their personal contacts. They rigorously screen for an "at cause" attitude, which is generally seen as being as important as a strong skill set and track record. They seek managers who, however experienced, are *hungry* for success, are willing to put their own financial upside at risk, and relish the challenge of transforming a company.

A PE firm may well conclude that the incumbent CEO of an acquired company is the right person to continue to lead it. This tends to be the case when the company is more or less on the right track and mainly needs to be taken to a new level of performance. In these circumstances, the PE firm looks to partner with the CEO. By contrast, when the company needs a turnaround, the acquiring PE firm often will conclude that some members of existing management lack either the skill or the will to succeed.

Even in relatively tradition-bound Europe, PE firms are breaking away from the old management buyout model, in which executives always came along with the purchase of a company. Two of the leading European PE firms that we've studied have replaced more than half of the senior management (including some CEOs) in their portfolio companies.

In going outside, PE firms look for managers with both the drive and the ability to make investments succeed. Rather than parachuting in an expert who is talented at, say, purchasing, the acquirers look for someone who is a proven team builder, understands the importance of building value quickly, and has demonstrated the ability to hit ambitious targets. (Think again of David Calhoun at VNU Group, and Michael Capellas, now at PE-owned First Data.) The individual with these "generalist" talents is then backed up with other senior executives, as well as expert technical advisers needed to reach their objectives. After appointing Bob Nardelli—with his proven track record for "hard driving" but little automotive experience—as CEO at Chrysler, Cerberus lost no time hiring proven automotive experts to support Nardelli. It brought on board Jim Press, the respected head of Toyota's North American operations, as head of sales, marketing, and product strategy; and Phil Murtaugh, widely credited with building GM's successful business in China, as head of Asia operations, where Chrysler intends to expand. It also kept Tom LaSorda, the former CEO under Daimler, as vice chairman and president.

Once the targeted individuals are on board, the challenge is to motivate them in the right directions. The most important way that PE firms recruit senior talent is to give them an equity position in their company that *grows when targets are hit over the life of the investment*. In other words, the management team may get 5 to 10 percent of the equity in the company going in and get the opportunity to earn another 20 percent, meaning that they get more than a quarter of the value of the company at the end of the (typical) three- to five-year investment period.

Obviously, this can amount to a significant payout—far more important than salaries and bonuses combined. Depending on the specific circumstances, it can involve dozens of people, which amounts to a broad base for impact. Rewards remain closely tied to performance.

In many cases, it turns out that hitting these targets requires hard work, but not magic. There may be great talent at the top. A great number of companies acquired by PE firms also have strong talent one or two levels down. (This is part of the PE firm's due diligence: *how much talent is resident in the organization?*) Once new incentives are put in place, these people tend to come to the fore.

PE firms take full advantage of these ambitious insiders—and, as necessary, complement them with outsiders. The company's new blueprint may involve a departure from standard operating procedures. Who—inside or outside—has the skill, guts, and drive to take the plunge?

PE firms, too, find ways to hold on to talent— even when that talent gets moved out of an acquired company. For example, they retain CEOs and other senior management by bringing them back into the PE firm or by appointing them to lead or otherwise help newly acquired portfolio companies. A good executive who led *Company A* may be able to serve newly acquired *Company B* in either an executive or a board position. In some cases, getting transplanted into an entirely new industry is enough to rekindle the thrill of the hunt in a senior manager.

## Case in Point: Converse

Going outside the industry in search of hungry managers was the order of the day when Perseus LLC and Infinity Associates purchased sneaker maker Converse out of bankruptcy in a court action for $117 million in 2001. Shortly after the acquisition, Perseus brought in Jack Boys, who previously had transformed The North Face into an outdoor-gear phenomenon. Boys brought with him a number of his colleagues from The North Face. Among other things, they shut down all U.S. manufacturing operations and used their North Face expertise in China to find quality suppliers and designers of shoes.

Converse made a big comeback and sales increased dramatically. Boys and his team recast Converse so effectively that rival Nike bought the company two years later for $305 million, netting Perseus six times its equity investment. Obviously, Nike decided that Boys deserved a lot of the credit for the turnaround: he was persuaded to stay on as CEO of Converse after the acquisition.

This is a good example of how PE firms network and keep in touch with talented senior managers; when the right opportunity comes along, they rally them in. Perseus knew Boys and his team, and had worked with them before at The North Face. It is also a good example of a brand that was long on potential but did not have enough talent to execute on that potential. Converse wasn't worth much to a buyer unless the buyer could supply the needed talent.

## PE Portfolio Companies and Their Boards

In addition to finding, landing, and motivating the right executive leadership, the PE owner is also attending to the composition and contributions of the company's board. Almost without exception, the best PE firms look to assemble what might be called a *value-added* board. This means two things. First, the board's members have skills that are of significant value to the management team in the operation of the company. They are active, talented participants. Second, and as an outgrowth of the first, they permit efficiency in the company's operations and governance. They minimize process and politics, and maximize action.

Suppose the CEO of a midsize PE-owned firm proposes to make a $200 million capital investment. Most likely, the board will see its job as determining whether or not this proposed investment fits with the full-potential thesis and the blueprint. The board is likely to include a number of people who have substantial firsthand experience with the product, market, or industry under discussion. The debate is likely to be knowledge and fact-based, and thus short and focused.

Nor does the discussion stop at the board table. In most PE-owned company settings, the CEO is in a continuing dialogue with members of the board—again, not for political reasons, but to obtain substantive, action-oriented guidance. Very little of the CEO's time is spent "bringing board members around"; most of it is spent drawing on their expertise.

Depending on the size and sophistication of the PE firm, there may also be a larger pool of expert advisers available to the CEO of a portfolio company. (GE's former head, Jack Welch, plays this role for Clayton, Dubilier & Rice.) These experts may participate in formal board reviews or in more one-off kinds of ways.

The key point is that all of these players are on the same page. It helps enormously, of course, that the PE firm's seats on the board generally control something like more than half of the voting stock. It helps, too, that the other non-PE members of the board have equity positions of various sizes. Everyone has the same incentives and is pulling in the same direction.

## Harnessing Talent in the Corporation

Let's look first at inside talent and then consider outside talent.

When it comes to assessing your insiders, try hard to smoke out and examine your own implicit assumptions. For example, sometimes senior-level executives assume that their junior people would prefer to "hide in the herd." In other words, the assumption is that they would prefer to be compensated on the basis of overall corporate performance rather than the performance of the unit over which they have bottom-line control.

Don't sell your existing people short. Certainly, there are, in your ranks, a certain number of entrepreneurial types who want their individual success at implementing the full-potential thesis and blueprint to be reflected in their personal compensation scheme. You need to find these people, set them up to succeed, and then reward them when they *do* succeed.

Maybe this sounds obvious, but in our experience, CEOs—especially CEOs who are in crisis mode—are inclined to think that the people who are already on the payroll are part of the problem rather than the solution. Yes, you have to be choosy, but you also have to be open to the great find in your midst. You have to be prepared to embrace that individual in whom the company has invested a great deal, who understands more about the current realities than any outsider could, and who may be ripe to help the company strike out in a new direction. In previous sections, we've encouraged you to keep your eyes open for potential allies. Here's where that list can come in handy.

Eventually, however, you might find that you need to go outside for some talent. Here is where you may find that you have trouble competing with your PE counterparts. As a CEO, you already understand the "economy of talent." Talent, like investment, gravitates toward good risk/reward opportunities. But while investors have the luxury of allocating their funds across multiple asset classes and in funds with different risk/reward profiles, most of us can only do one job. Therefore, jobs that present opportunities that lie above the risk/reward line—such as those at the top PE firms and their portfolio companies— tend to attract a disproportionate amount of the available talent.

So what can you do to overcome the economics of talent and level the playing field? First, as we have discussed when talking incentives and bonuses, you can ensure that your financial offer to talent is at least in line with the risks you are asking them to take. What does this mean? It means you have to pay close to market value for the skills you require. Don't be handcuffed by tradition-bound notions of pay grades and antiquated hierarchical systems. Get market data on the alternatives talented people have and make sure your compensation package is competitive.

Second, you can play up the non-financial elements of the rewards that you offer. Depending on the specifics of the manager and your circumstances, these elements can make a big difference in your target's calculations. Does your company's mission overlap with the candidate's values? Does your location appeal to him or her? Does the prospect of extensive travel— or the complete absence of travel—hold strong appeal for this individual? Do you have appealing, challenging, talented colleagues who, through their inspiring example, can help close the deal? How about your *own* example? Why did your board bet on you? If the answer includes your ability to inspire and motivate, this is the time to call on those skills.

As noted in the previous section, you will need to find ways to include contingent compensation in your packages. But if the contingent piece of the compensation is large enough—and if the targets are ambitious but realistic—you have nothing to apologize for. To put it bluntly, you need to find people who are more interested in opportunities than guarantees. To do so, you will have to scramble, invent, and push against the tide. A few effective ways top corporations do this:

- Explore "phantom equity" and other mechanisms that have been introduced in recent years by companies who are trying to solve exactly these kinds of problems. Phantom equity refers to plans (such as phantom stock or stock appreciation rights) that provide employees with a cash or stock payout based on the increase in the company's stock value, but without granting them an actual ownership stake in the company.

- Look for people who aren't yet infected with the "lifer" mentality.

- Look for people in lower-paying sectors who don't yet know what they're worth and would welcome the chance to sign on with a company (like yours) that's clearly on the move. Give your hires extraordinary responsibilities and superb support, to increase the odds that they'll win. And when they *do* win, treat them the way PE firms treat their winners: with extraordinary generosity.

The role of boards in a public-company setting is a topic that could fill a book—and already has, many times over. In the wake of the Enron, WorldCom, Adelphia, Parmalat, Ahold, and other scandals, and in the wake of the passage of corporate governance regulations such as Sarbanes-Oxley in the United States and Higgs in the United Kingdom, public-company boards have new sets of rules that they are supposed to live by. They are supposed to be more skeptical, more independent, and generally less under the influence of the CEO—whom they are supposed to be more prepared to dispose of when circumstances seem to warrant it. They are supposed to be tougher on compensation issues, on audit-related issues, and on protecting the shareholders' interests in general.

One of our clients in a public-company context set out to change his board, which he described bluntly as a "disaster." Over the course of three years, he moved the non-contributors out and replaced them with substantially more effective people.

If your board is similarly challenged, consider making a similar transition—of course, playing by the rules of the game. But consider *departing* from the informal rules of the game when it comes to signing up new people. Instead of recruiting people who generally see the world the same way you do, consider recruiting bona fide experts in your business or industry—or in an area where you see trends developing that might impact your business. Meanwhile, consider setting up subcommittees that draw on the best board talent that is currently available to you. Focus those subcommittees on your key initiatives. Augment them with external resources, as needed and as appropriate. Build an internal resource that understands one or more key components of the blueprint. Find ways to get your board members to ask critical questions *sooner*—which should render decision-making down the road much more efficient. Instruct them in the intricacies of debt levels (a subject to which we'll return in the next section). If they are going to make or validate the crucial calls, they absolutely have to be attuned to your thinking. Share this memo with them. Share anything else that helps them think about the PE disciplines and how they can adopt similar tools and techniques to enhance the company's value.

Initiate a discussion with the board about earnings forecasts: *do we want to play this game, or not?* When James Kilts took over Gillette in 2001, the company had missed its forecasts fourteen quarters in a row, with a predictable impact on the share price. Working with his board, Kilts set his sights on the middle term—meaning, more than the next few months—stopped issuing earnings guidance, and incurred the predictable outcry from Wall Street. But two years later, with costs cut and market share on the rise, free cash flow had doubled, and Wall Street was happy. It would not have been possible had Kilts not trained his board to think in the strategic middle term.

Outside the United States, of course, boards play by still different rules, which require very different actions on the part of the CEO. In Japan and Korea, for example, boards are viewed as repositories of general business experience, and board seats are viewed as a way of recognizing past achievements. German boards tend to be coalitions of labor and major shareholders, and not generally involved in strategy setting. These models, and others around the world, are very different from the PE model—and therefore very difficult to bring into line with the PE perspectives that we have outlined above.

As usual, there's no easy answer. Keep looking for ways to get your board members tuned in to the competitive realities—which are, or should be, a universal focus—and encourage them to think hard about the PE phenomenon that is sweeping the world.

## Summary: Harness the Talent

Acquire, retain, and motivate results-oriented people.

Share equity with key people.

Reward "boldness and success."

Invent creative compensation tools, tying equity to what you actually do—for example, phantom equity.

Assemble a value-added board—with bona fide experts.

*Work* the board—make it decisive and efficient:

- Set up board subcommittees focused on key initiatives.

- Find ways to get the board to ask critical questions sooner.

# Make Equity Sweat

Almost every business needs capital to grow. How do the best PE players think about equity, and what can you learn from that perspective? Simply stated, they embrace leverage as a relatively cheap capital structure. If they need $100 for growth, they (typically) finance that sum with $70 of debt and $30 of equity. Then they focus on generating cash, which they can use to either (1) pay down debt or (2) invest in productive ways. This, in turn, means that PE firms and their portfolio companies aggressively manage their capital—working capital, capital expenditures, fixed assets—forcing the business to be as efficient as possible: *making it sweat*. They focus intensively on their balance sheet.

Most traditional corporations take an inverse approach. (On average, companies acquired by PE firms shoot for 70 percent debt and 30 percent equity; in contrast, U.S. public companies are capitalized with 40 percent debt on average, while European companies are capitalized with 35 percent debt on average.) Many traditional corporations fund much of their capital expenditures out of cash or with equity. They set relatively low hurdles for their investments, on the theory that internally funded initiatives are "cheap." (They aren't.) Many companies minimize leverage, on the theory that keeping a lid on debt limits their debt-service exposure and keeps more options open to them. While they certainly strive for efficient and economical operations, these companies aren't forced to wring every available dollar out of the system to make their (modest) debt pay. They tip their hats to their balance sheets and pay close attention to their income statements.

This topic—managing how the operations and growth of the business are funded—presents some of the sharpest contrasts between PE-owned companies and more traditional ones. It is also a realm in which you have much discretion—although if you choose to emulate the PE approach, you will almost certainly have a lot of explaining to do to your more conservative constituents. With that in mind, let's dig into the notion of "making equity sweat" a little more deeply.

## Why PE Firms Love Cash

As noted, PE players look at their balance sheets not as static indicators of performance, but as dynamic tools for growth. One critical component of this approach is to *aggressively manage down working capital.* This may sound like Finance 101, but in fact, in a private equity environment, managing down working capital can be an indispensable part of the larger value creation formula.

In a leveraged business, managing cash always takes priority over managing earnings. Why? Let's look at a simplified example. PE owners generally use EBITDA as a measure of cash flow. They then look carefully at below-the-line costs to understand the real cash-generation potential of a business. Let's assume that EBITDA is $125. We need to deduct three things from this number to arrive at the real cash generation of the business: the total debt-service requirement (principal and interest), working capital as a percent of sales times the planned annual sales growth, and the capital expenditures needed to continue to run and grow the business.

Let's say in our fictional example that the annual debt service is $50. Let's further say that the working capital as a percent of sales is 30 percent, and that next year's growth in sales is budgeted at $100. That means that $30 (30 percent of $100) of cash will be required to fund budgeted growth. Finally, let's assume that capital expenditures are $10 (maintenance expenditures plus required expenditures to fund sales growth). Adding those three deductions ($50 + $30 + $10) means that this business has $90 of cash requirements, and prior-year EBITDA of $125 to fund them. In this example, therefore, the *real cash creation* is $35. Bear in mind that no picture of cash flow is static, but depends on changes in market forces, competitors and customers. Thus, smart PE investors and CEOs measure the cash-generation potential of their businesses on a regular basis.

Looking carefully at these three deductions—again, debt service, working capital requirements for sales growth, and capital expenditures—you can quickly see that only one of these can be actively managed in the near term: working capital requirements (debt is relatively fixed, and capital expenditure has both a maintenance and a "growth" component; we'll address the growth component below). If you need to find more cash on a sustainable basis, you need to drive down your working capital. Going back to our example, if through better inventory management and receivables/payables management we can move our business from a working capital ratio of 30 percent of new sales to 20 percent of new sales, that will save $10 of cash and increase the business's cash creation from $35 to $45—in other words, a *30 percent increase* in cash creation as a result of using our working capital more efficiently.

In a leveraged situation, cash is king, and active managers also need to make their capital expenditures sweat to minimize their cash requirements. Obviously, not every industry structure is the same, and capital expenditures are less relevant in some businesses, but the principle is the same. Most PE firms ask a very specific and focused version of the following question: *If I put a dollar into this capital project, am I going to get three dollars back out?* In other words, they apply exactly the same discipline to their capital expenditures as they did to their initial investment in the company.

Finally, active managers make the physical capital on the balance sheet work harder. They find new ways to convert traditionally fixed assets into sources of financing. They eliminate unproductive capital by selling equipment or by closing facilities. And they divest underperforming businesses or divisions. The capital released can be redeployed to more productive uses.

## Two Quick Cases:
## Punch Taverns Group
## and Mueller Water Products

Let's look briefly at two cases in which PE firms acquired companies and set out to make equity sweat.

The first involves TPG, which in 1999 acquired Punch Taverns Group, a chain of 1,470 pubs in the United Kingdom.[15] A few months later, TPG and Punch made a bold move to acquire Allied Domecq's thirty-five hundred pubs—squaring off against a much larger suitor, Whitbread, in what turned out to be a hotly contested bid. TPG and Punch outmaneuvered Whitbread and won the deal, in part by working Punch's balance sheet to lower the cost of financing the acquisition.

TPG's financing consisted of a £1.6 billion bridge loan, which it later refinanced by securitizing its newly acquired pub assets. Thanks to the stable and predictable nature of pub revenues, Punch was able to isolate the rents it earned on real estate (an important source of cash flow) and package them as real estate investment securities that could be sold to investors. This collaterized debt offering proved attractive for investors as well as sellers.

This innovative use of the balance sheet helped achieve a more efficient capital structure, saving some £30 million in annual interest costs. In combination with focused operating improvements, it also enabled TPG to restore growth to a business that for years had posted flat to declining sales. In fact, despite the maturity of the industry as a whole, Punch's pub revenues began increasing at more than 7 percent annually.

Case number two: in 1999, DLJ Merchant Banking (the PE arm of Credit Suisse First Boston) purchased Mueller Water Products—an old-line maker of fire hydrants, high-pressure valves, and fittings—from Tyco for $938 million, of which just $231 million was equity. Closing uncompetitive foundries and innovating leaner manufacturing methods freed up cash for acquisitions, which collectively helped boost revenue from $865 million in 2001 to $1 billion in 2004. In mid-2005, Walter Industries agreed to buy Mueller for almost $2 billion, earning the PE owner a nearly fivefold return on their equity investment in about six years.

## What Squeezing Equity Means for You

The first and most basic question you need to answer, as you think about the PE approach to financing a business, is what level of debt you and your constituencies are comfortable with, keeping in mind the cash a company must have on hand for various business needs, including potential acquisitions. After all, public companies have no recourse to a parent fund for needed cash, and need to proceed with caution. Debt is a relatively inexpensive form of financing, but—as we've seen—only if you can manage your receivables, ride herd on your inventory, and otherwise manage your working capital, at the same time that you discipline your capital expenditures and work hard the fixed assets on your balance sheet.

Next, get an accurate handle on *exactly where and when in the process you begin to make cash*. We had an interesting conversation with a CEO recently on the subject of cash management. We asked him what his principal pay-down plus interest costs amounted to (numbers are proportionally correct but disguised).

"Fifty million," he responded.

"How much revenue growth are you going to have next year?"

"We're going for $100 million," he said.

"So you've already told us that your working capital is 40 percent of sales. That means—figuring 40 percent of $100 million—that you're going to have to add $40 million of cash in working capital to finance that $100 million. What's your cap ex?"

"Ten million," he replied.

"OK," we said. "You're telling us that you have to pay $50 million in debt, $40 million to fund sales growth, and another $10 million in cap ex. So unless your EBITDA is more than $100 million, you're losing cash. In other words, you begin to make cash at over $100 million."

He was a bit surprised by the implications of his financial structure—but ultimately embraced the notion of not just looking at EBITDA, but looking below the line as well to properly forecast cash generation. Once again: *cash is king.* This CEO subsequently found ways to squeeze his working capital down from $40 million to $25 million, thereby bringing his EBITDA breakeven down by 15 percent.

This is life in a leveraged environment. If you go this route, you are likely to hear a lot of voices cautioning you to be more conservative, especially as liquidity cycles are not predictable. We touched on that topic earlier. You are also likely to hear grumblings about how a greedy corporate center is unfairly squeezing the divisions. That is one perspective. The other perspective is to say, *This is how we should be running our business in any case. We are in competition with PE firms and other active investors who will eat our lunch if we continue to be relaxed about our use of equity.*

Now let's think about how your company approaches its capital expenditures. Many companies go through what they deem rigorous capital budgeting exercises—but most of these are less rigorous than first meets the eye. Many capital plans forecast fast and fabulous paybacks, project by project—but if you look at the balance sheet and the cash flow, you find that many of these projects only start to pay off long after the forecasted date. Some projects never pay off. In some cases, digging deeper reveals even more serious problems: even at good companies, as many as one in five capital expenditures winds up returning *nothing*.

There are companies that are even less rigorous than the above depiction. They tacitly view their capital budget as a cost of doing business. All sorts of things, ranging from maintenance to growth capital, are lumped together under this loose umbrella. If sales go up 10 percent, it's assumed that the capital budget will also go up by something like 10 percent. It gets budgeted, and—not surprisingly—it gets spent.

The point is that smart managers must think holistically, over time, on the basis of their full-potential thesis and blueprint. Say you buy a billion-dollar business, putting in $300 million in equity. You do so on the basis of a certain full-potential thesis (as described in our earlier sections). Over the subsequent five years, you double the size of that business to $2 billion. But how much additional equity have you invested? Let's say it's another $300 million. *You have to hold that second $300 million to the same return standards that you held the first $300 million to*—otherwise, you are diluting your overall return. You have to make sure that the component parts of that second $300 million conform to the blueprint. Better yet: make

100

new investments with an eye toward "moving the needle"—that is, aiming for an even *better* overall performance by refreshing the strategic due diligence and, as a result, optimizing key initiatives.

Then, make sure that the individual investments are *closely monitored for performance*. Make sure there is a closed feedback loop on each of them, so you get early readings about unrealistic assumptions that have sneaked into the plan. Is the pricing you're getting from customers significantly lower than anticipated? Is something else going wrong? If so, intervene! Don't let any of your investments fall into that one-in-five, zero-return scrap heap.

One practical way for CEOs to discipline their capital expenditures is to play an active role in the capital allocation process. Warren Buffet believes that capital allocation decisions are the most important ones he makes: "Charles T. Munger, Berkshire Hathaway's vice chairman, and I really have only two jobs. One is to attract and keep outstanding managers to run our various operations. The other is capital allocation."[16] Though Berkshire Hathaway is fundamentally different from many corporations, we firmly believe these principles have outstanding merit for any business.

Finally, make sure you have taken stock of your fixed assets and think hard about whether they belong on your balance sheet. For example, it has become common in many countries for airlines to improve balance sheet health by selling fleets and leasing back planes, and in the retail and hospitality sector to sell off sites and rent facilities. Also, think hard about divesting the businesses that are either underperforming or may be worth more to others.

It all adds up to a mind-set: *Every dollar of equity is precious, and I have to maximize the return on that dollar.* By adding leverage to the balance sheet, you are—by definition—making equity scarcer and more valuable. The same is true with managing your working capital aggressively, managing the capital budgeting process in a highly disciplined way, and monetizing unproductive assets.

Every dollar of equity is precious. Make it sweat!

## Monday Morning Matters: Make Equity Sweat

Embrace leverage.

Focus on cash generation (to make debt pay).

Aggressively manage:

- Working capital

  - Receivables/payables

- Inventory

- Capital expenditures

- Other balance sheet assets

  - Unproductive equipment/facilities

  - Businesses/divisions that are under-performing or worth more to others

  - Traditionally fixed assets converted as sources of financing

Invest capital with discipline:

- Think of your *new* capital investments as important as *original* investments.

- Think of capital as also financed with debt.

- Measure against realistic expectations.

Use new investments to "move the needle."

# Foster a Results-Oriented Mind-set

Fostering a results-oriented mind-set is about creating repeatable, sustainable processes in your company that will spur performance improvements again and again. Most businesses hit bumps in the road from time to time, but if you rigorously apply the five lessons we have discussed so far to your own company, you will ingrain the right behaviors into the organization. After some time passes, these right behaviors become the culture. *Culture* is an overused word, but we use it to mean the right managers with a bias for questioning the status quo, getting the facts, taking action, and ultimately driving this "at cause" behavior throughout the organization.

We don't know the specifics of the mind-set that prevails in your business today. But our experience suggests strongly that too many companies have an operating culture that is stuck in the past and ill equips them for the present—let alone the future. In the current business environment, increasingly impacted by PE firms and other activist investors, people demand *performance*. They demand *value creation*. They are impatient with results that are only average (or worse).

Most of what goes into creating such a mind-set has been included in the previous sections:

- Define the full potential.

- Develop the blueprint.

- Accelerate performance.

- Harness the talent.

- Make equity sweat.

In this final section, we will add five more prescriptions that can help move your company's mind-set strongly toward results.

## Make It a Repeatable Formula

There's been quite a bit written in recent years about "learning organizations." In our experience, the best PE firms are excellent learning organizations. They put forward their theory of full potential, blueprint it, test it, monitor it, figure out what's wrong, recalibrate, and move forward again. Over time, these PE firms get better and better at what they do, on both a business and on an industry basis. They develop successful formulas that they (1) can repeat within a business and (2) can replicate outside the business.

You don't have to be a PE firm to achieve repeatability. We often cite Nike as an example of a public company that has established and ingrained relentless repeatability into its business model. Nike began as a "performance" basketball shoe company, and has transformed itself over time to a lifestyle company. Underneath that transition was a very concrete, repeatable formula that Nike used to set its blueprint, and that it revisited over time as it went into new sports—from running to volleyball, to tennis, to basketball, to soccer, to golf. Nike begins by establishing a leading position in athletic shoes in the target market. Next, it launches a clothing line endorsed by the sport's top athletes—like Tiger Woods, whose $100 million deal in 1996 gave Nike the visibility it needed to get traction in golf apparel and accessories. Expanding into new categories allows the company to forge new distribution channels and lock in suppliers. Then it starts to feed higher-margin equipment into the market: balls, then irons first, in the case of golf clubs, and subsequently drivers. In the final step, Nike moves beyond the U.S. market to global distribution. To organize for continued growth, Nike recently realigned its businesses around key sports categories:

men's training, women's fitness, running, basketball, soccer, and sports culture.

Looking for the right adjacencies, and jumping into them with a "new but related" blueprint, is a key component of the results-oriented mind-set. The best PE firms do it all the time—but as the Nike experience demonstrates, so can you.[17]

## Demand Accountability

We haven't talked much so far about CEOs who travel in the "opposite" direction: that is, from heading up PE-owned firms to heading up traditional firms. The most common refrain we hear from these individuals, when they start figuring out their new environment, is that no one is accountable, but that's not the full story. Of course, the top management team is ultimately responsible. The stronger that team, the more likely it is that all accountability will "drift upward" toward the corner offices. The unfortunate result? We have too often seen the emergence of initiatives, and sometimes even whole divisions, in which no manager feels true ownership of results. It is no surprise that these types of organizations tend to end up being "at effect" versus "at cause."

As we have previously discussed, among the best PE investors, this is unacceptable. Senior managers have to push accountability down to its most effective level, which most of the time doesn't mean you. (CEOs, as they say, can't "do all the doing.") The general managers of your business units have to feel that they are on the hook to deliver the results. The people who own the initiatives and whose names are on the actions in the blueprint have to feel that they are equally on the hook.

As the CEOs traveling in the "opposite" direction have discovered, this type of accountability is less common in public companies, but often simply because not enough emphasis has been placed on the need to have it. Peter Brabeck has recently pushed accountability to the limit at Nestlé by eliminating not just job levels, but also job descriptions: "I tell my people, 'Here is the framework. I want you to spend 50 percent of your time doing what you are supposed to do, but spend 50 percent on telling me how *you* can create more value,'" he says.[18] He is doing this across functions and grades throughout the company, taking the approach, as noted earlier, right down to the very simplest jobs on the factory floor, where he has eliminated supervisors and put workers in charge of monitoring their own output and developing their own plans for improvement. Does it work? In the past decade, Nestlé's employee productivity has climbed almost 20 percent and cost of goods sold fallen from 52 percent to 41 percent.

Brabeck's approach to continuous improvement flows directly from his full-potential vision of improving operational performance and the blueprint that followed. Note that the full-potential thesis and the blueprint *never go away*. They are merely refreshed and updated over the life of the business.

## Articulate and Communicate

Your job as CEO is about *leading*. And when you lead an organization into change, you assume the significant burden of making sense out of it all for everyone else. This is especially true when times "feel good" and the organization feels no sense of urgency, yet you have decided to take it from what we referred to earlier as "satisfactory underperformance" to "full potential." People always respond better to unplanned change—that is, crises and disasters—than they do to planned change.

Your job is to explain why business as usual won't work anymore and why aspiring to create change for the better is the best plan for all. In some cases this may be a formalization of many things already going on inside your organization. In others it may be more revolution than evolution. Does your company have principles, aspirations, and nontangible goals? Of course it does. Do your people have personal goals and ideals? Certainly. Your job is to articulate why and then persuade your people that the organization has a *far better chance* of achieving those goals if they adopt change, in whatever language best suits your company and your own style. Collectively, you will create more jobs, and more opportunities. You will deliver more authority, and greater financial rewards, to the people who are *actually creating the value*. In our experience, people respond with enormous energy and enthusiasm to *that* proposition. Clearly this is not a one-time speech.

And creative tools for reiterating your message are more numerous than ever. Many effective CEOs have become experts at mixing the latest technology with a human touch. Some create special intranets to track the progress of blueprint initiatives and/or send e-mail updates. Others articulate vocally through phone messages and teleconferences; and still others add visual urgency and enthusiasm for special messages via videoconferencing and face-to-face interactions in "Town Hall"–style meetings at offices and plants. Each of these tools can effectively build enthusiasm for the vision of full potential and its blueprint for change.

The best communicators find new and different ways to get the vision for change and its milestones across to as many internal audiences as possible. Indeed, they consider it one of their most critical jobs and tirelessly drive home the message, again and again.

## Set the Striking Example

What are the visible steps that you can take to make the point that this is no longer business as usual? What changes can you implement today that will have both high symbolic value and also a real impact?

For one, you can set a striking example for your team, as did the new CEO of an old-line industrial company whose stultified organization was killing the business. Under the new CEO's leadership, doors were removed from the offices ("so that people would have to communicate with each other"). Several internal boards, each of which met regularly, were eliminated. The CEO and his management team called meetings whenever they needed to talk about issues—and kept them short, rather than reverting to the old schedule of daylong meetings every six weeks. And the new CEO repeatedly visited all the major plants and offices, whereas his predecessor stuck largely to headquarters. Every one of these actions was a cue: *things are going to be different around here*. And they were. People throughout the organization noticed the new behavior and started acting accordingly.

## Reset the Standard

Resetting standards is simply a plea for keeping an edge on the blueprint and—as a result—on the results orientation of the company. Smart PE firms are *constantly* moving the goalposts in the direction of higher performance and better results.

As mentioned earlier, we are often called in by PE firms to do a new due diligence on properties that they already own. Why? First, of course, they want to make sure that the current blueprint still makes sense—a defensive mode. But second, and probably more important, they want to make sure that they're not missing any opportunities for even better performance. Often, the diligence turns up exactly those kinds of opportunities. Remember, the goal here is not to make budget. The goal is to achieve "full potential." These are very different aims!

The result is a *reset*—usually not a change in course, but an intensification of ongoing activities. If we can see a way to go from A to A+, we're *going* there. We'll highlight this in our concluding section.

## Monday Morning Matters:
## Foster a Results-Oriented Mind-set

Make it a repeatable formula.

Demand accountability.

Articulate and communicate.

Set the striking example.

Reset the standard.

---

# Conclusion

Let's close with a last look at the two companies we used as examples in our opening section. Nestlé and Crown Castle represent well-run organizations that demonstrate how all of these PE lessons can be applied, regardless of ownership model.

At Nestlé, one can look back at Brabeck's original full-potential thesis and cite facts that show he in large part arrived (before his announcement in late 2007 that he would name a successor as CEO in 2008). For starters, Nestlé's share price, once trading at a discount, transformed itself into a premium, having boosted market capitalization 3.5 times to more than SF 200 billion in the last ten years. By fall 2007, it had exceeded its original goal for total shareholder return (TSR) by achieving a TSR of 350 percent. How did Nestlé fair on the four original initiatives, the four "pillars," that Brabeck mapped out? The numbers cited above probably speak for themselves. Given Nestlé's size and complex number of businesses, and since we have used examples from Nestlé throughout the memo, we will just summarize a few highlights.

- **Operational performance improvement:** Nestlé achieved $3 billion of cost savings in the first three years alone, selling or closing more than two hundred factories. Overall, the company's productivity, expressed in sales per employee, rose almost 20 percent from 1997 to 2006. In addition, thanks in large part to GLOBE penetrating 80 percent or more of Nestlé's local market organizations, Brabeck estimated that Nestlé gained a five-year jump on expansion over competitors owing to better, quicker decisions and dissemination of best practices.

- **Innovating and renovating products:** As mentioned, Nestlé has largely renewed its product portfolio across all divisions. It also built new, and now leading, businesses in bottled water, pet food, and ice cream. At the same time, it divested businesses that could not differentiate themselves through R&D. In the process, the company has hit its *organic* growth objective of 5 to 6 percent per year with improved margins.

- **Distribution "whenever, wherever, however":**
  The new distribution model has diversified
  Nestlé from a reliance mostly on major, global
  distributors such as Wal-Mart and Carrefour to
  only 20 percent of its sales today going through
  the top ten retailers. For example, in its confec-
  tionary category alone, 50 percent of Nestlé's
  sales now occur through nontraditional channels
  such as stadiums, cinemas, and street vendors.

- **Consumer communications:**  Brabeck, as
  hoped, saw spending on traditional television
  advertising fall from 95 percent to about 65
  percent, and interactive consumer outreach
  rise and fill the gap.

- **Resetting the bar:**  Finally, in the past few
  years, Nestlé has begun to reset the bar. Most
  critically, the company is well down the road
  on incorporating nutritional elements into
  traditional products. Brabeck has created a
  stand-alone nutrition division that handles
  infant, baby, clinical, and performance nutrition as well as weight management. All the
  while, he continues to push the disciplines we
  described throughout the memo to propel
  Nestlé's huge traditional and new businesses
  around the world. The vision now? For Nestlé

to be recognized as more than just a leading *food and beverage* company, and instead to be acknowledged as the world's most respected *nutrition, health, and wellness* company.

Finally, let's return to what became of Crown Castle *after* it went public. By the early 1990s, the company had built a portfolio of over eleven thousand towers in the United States and also owned broadcast transmission towers for the BBC in the United Kingdom as well as some towers in Australia. In late 2001, with the "growth by acquisition" phase largely over, CEO John Kelly held a meeting with all key senior managers to discuss the crucial issues facing the company, and kicked off an effort to redefine the business's full potential and build a robust blueprint to achieve it.

After digging into the facts and debating alternatives, senior managers zeroed in on a few key initiatives. First, they made the tough decision to divest the U.K. broadcast network. The U.K. business operated a largely analog, broadcast transmission network from end to end, which made it vulnerable to technology shifts (e.g., analog broadcast television migrating to digital). It was a far different business with a very different risk profile than the U.S. tower business, whose core function was to lease space to wireless carriers, thus generating long-term, predictable revenues and cash flows that were far less vulnerable to changes in technology. Senior managers decided that the U.K. business, while attractive in its own right, was sufficiently different from the core U.S. business that it would provide more of a distraction and a drain on scarce management resources in the long run, and was not an optimum allocation of Crown Castle's capital resources.

Then, to encourage the maximum lease-up rate on its towers, Crown Castle developed services and bundles that would sway wireless providers to put incremental antennas on its towers over competitors' towers. Last, the company aggressively invested in its systems infrastructure to be able to deliver on these value-added services. Crown Castle became the first player in the industry to offer full schematics of towers with precise location information, blueprints, and satellite photos. Crown Castle was also the only company in the industry to develop a lease-forecasting tool that reliably predicts future demand on a tower-by-tower basis.

In 2006, the company decided to reset its take on the full potential of the business. While the landscape had not changed much, the senior managers saw an opportunity in increasing the scale of the business. In 2007, Crown Castle announced the acquisition of Global Signal, nearly doubling its tower portfolio to over twenty-four thousand towers. So what has the payoff been? Leading an industry that some skeptics were once doubtful could succeed, Crown Castle saw its stock price increase from a low of $1 in 2002 to a high of $40 at the end October 2007. During the same five-year period, Crown Castle invested over $2 billion, largely with borrowed funds, to reduce its fully diluted shares outstanding by approximately 30 percent because it believed in the underlying value of the cash flow from its tower assets. Such disciplines, used by the top PE firms, played a substantial role in driving Crown Castle's success.

# Lessons

To summarize the lessons from private equity that CEOs cannot afford to ignore:

- **Define the full potential:** The target is increased equity value—how to turn $1 of equity value today into $3, $4, or $5 tomorrow. *Strategic due diligence* is the way to set the number, and growing cash flow by pursuing a few core initiatives is the way to get there.

- **Develop the blueprint:** The blueprint is the road map for reaching your full potential—the *who*, *what*, *when*, *where*, and *how*. It zeroes in on the few core initiatives and delineates a step-by-step plan to turn them into results. The emphasis is on measurable actions.

- **Accelerate performance:** This involves molding the organization to the blueprint, matching talent to key initiatives, and getting people to own them. It also involves creating a rigorous program to achieve your ends—one that combines tools, discipline, and the monitoring of a few key metrics.

- **Harness the talent:** This requires creating the right incentives to recruit, retain, and motivate your best talent—and get them to think and act like owners. It also requires assembling a decisive and efficient board.

- **Make equity sweat:** The challenge is to embrace *LBO economics*. This calls for managing working capital aggressively, disciplining capital expenditures, and working the balance sheet hard.

- **Foster a results-oriented mind-set:** The goal is to inculcate PE disciplines so that they become part of the company's culture and create a repeatable formula for achieving results.

# Notes

1. See, for example, "The Economic Impact of Private Equity in the UK 2006," BVCA, November 2006, http://www.bvca.co.uk/doc.php?id=549.

2. "U.S. Firm Buys into Shenzen Bank," *People's Daily Online*, June 3, 2004, http://english.people.com.cn/200406/03/eng20040603_145247.html.

3. Tim Higgins, "Cerberus to Purchase 80% Chrysler Stake: UAW Chief Supports Deal," *Detroit Free Press*, May 14, 2007, http://www.freep.com/apps/pbcs.dll/article?AID=/20070514/BUSINESS01/70514006.

4. Steve Schaubert and Mark Gottfredson, *The Breakthrough Imperative: How the Best Managers Get Outstanding Results* (New York: HarperCollins, forthcoming).

5. "Change Artist" interview with Peter Brabeck-Letmathe and Chris Johnson, CNN, April 2007.

6. Orit Gadiesh, interview with Peter Brabeck-Letmathe. August 21, 2007.

7. A more exhaustive list of PE firm diligence will include an accounting review, legal review, review of other liabilities (pension, OSHA, etc.). In developing markets (such as in India), the list also will include background diligence on the senior management who are likely to stay.

8. See Chris Bierly, Graham Elton, and Chul-Joon Park, "Private Equity's New Path to Profits," *Bain Brief*, December 2006.

9. See Geoffrey Cullinan, Jean-Marc Le Roux, and Rolf-Magnus Weddigen, "When to Walk Away from a Deal," *Harvard Business Review,* April 2004.

10. Eric Dash, "Job-hopping," *New York Times*, July 20, 2007.

11. See Sunny Yi and Chul-Joon Park, "Turbocharging Asian Turnarounds," *Harvard Business Review*, June 2006.

12. Paul Rogers, Tom Holland, and Dan Haas, "Value Acceleration Lessons from the Private Equity Masters," *Harvard Business Review*, June 2002.

13. For more on RAPID, see Paul Rogers and Marcia Blenko, "Who Has the D? How Clear Decision Roles Enhance Organizational Performance," *Harvard Business Review*, January 2006.

14. "Change Artist" interview with Peter Brabeck-Letmathe and Chris Johnson, CNN, April 2007.

15. Paul Rogers, Tom Holland, and Dan Haas, "Value Acceleration Lessons from the Private Equity Masters," *Harvard Business Review*, June 2002.

16. From Warren Buffet and Lawrence A. Cunningham, *The Essays of Warren Buffet: Lessons for Corporate America* (Durham, NC: Carolina Academic Press, 1997).

17. Described at length in Chris Zook's book *Beyond the Core: Expand Your Market Without Abandoning Your Roots* (Boston: Harvard Business School Press, 2004).

18. "Change Artist" interview with Peter Brabeck-Letmathe and Chris Johnson, CNN, April 2007.

# About the Authors

Orit Gadiesh is a global expert on management and corporate strategy. Ms Gadiesh, chairman, Bain & Company, has worked with hundreds of CEOs and senior executives of major international companies on strategy development and the implementation of change within the corporation. She splits her time on active client work between North America, Europe, and Asia.

Gadiesh, who has been named to *Fortune* magazine's "Most Powerful Women in Business" and to *Forbes* magazine's "The 100 Most Powerful Women in the World," is a frequent conference speaker and contributor to global business publications such as *The Wall Street Journal, The Financial Times, Forbes, Fortune, Far East Economic Review, The WEF Global Agenda, Le Monde,* and *Harvard Business Review*.

Prior to joining Bain & Company, Gadiesh served in the office of the Deputy Chief of Staff of the Israeli Army. She lives with her husband in Paris and Boston.

## About the Authors

Hugh MacArthur, partner, Bain & Company, is an expert on alternative investing and head of Bain's Global Private Equity practice. He advises private equity funds in performing strategic due diligence on targets and on how to improve the performance of their portfolio companies across many industries. He also consults to private equity funds themselves on matters such as asset class strategy, geographic expansion, fund raising strategy, organizational effectiveness, and fund operations. MacArthur has served as Bain & Company's own Chief Investment Officer, overseeing portfolios of investments in private equity deals.

MacArthur has authored on private equity value creation, post-acquisition strategies, and the state of the industry in publications around the globe including *The Wall Street Journal, The Financial Times, The Economic Times* of India, *China Daily, Forbes.com, The Deal, Buyouts and London Business School's* Business Strategy Review. He lives with his wife and children in Weston, Massachusetts.

Catherine Lemire, manager of Bain's Global Private Equity practice, and Bain partners Chris Bierly, Graham Elton, Dan Haas, Chul-Joon Park and Sri Rajan contributed research and content to this book. Jeff Cruikshank, a writer and author based in Milton, Massachusetts, served as collaborating writer.